AN INVITATION TO PUBLIC RELATIONS

AN INVITATION TO PUBLIC RELATIONS

(Seventy-one per cent said weasel)

SIMON MOORE

CASSELL

Cassell
Wellington House
125 Strand
London WC2R 0BB

127 West 24th Street
New York
NY 10011

First published 1996

British Library Cataloguing-in-Publication Data
A catalogue record for this book is available from the British Library

ISBN   0-304-33810-9 (hardback)
        0-304-33811-7 (paperback)

Typeset by Stephen Wright, the Rainwater Consultancy, Longworth, Oxfordshire

Printed and bound in Great Britain by Redwood Books Ltd, Trowbridge, Wilts.

Contents

Preface and Acknowledgements

'We have invented nothing,' murmured Picasso, stumbling into the light after viewing the cave paintings at Lascaux. I, too, have invented nothing. I have offered no models proving this that or any other aspect of public relations; I have speculated, in general terms, on the future. This book is written from a different premise: what makes public relations an engaging and worthwhile subject for the newcomer to study?

If I were invited to meet this subject for the first time, I would have four main questions in mind: is it creative enough to bring pleasure to my work? Will I find myself pushing against any moral or ethical boundaries? What of value lies beneath the surface? And how valid are the claims made for this subject by its practitioners?

In answering these questions I have considered current practice, ethics, history, and what are often called 'case studies' – accounts of public relations programmes drawn from my experiences as a practitioner, and more particularly from the wonderful archive of public-relations programmes kindly donated to the College of St Mark and St John, Plymouth, England, by the International Public Relations Association (IPRA) through the generous efforts of Professor Sam Black. The phrase 'case studies' bothers me: it has the sense of a project isolated in space and time, suggesting a selected facet of public relations – perhaps ethics – or more often than not a specific application. I have risked a diverse approach to 'case studies', taking them from the immediate present (some are known to academics, others of necessity heavily disguised, most are less well known and undisguised), from different countries and from the distant past. I have set them together to see what we might learn about the evolution and creative power of the field. Until we view public relations as universally as we view communications, we will be unable to understand its potency.

I wish to thank those persons and institutions who have worked to keep me on course, especially Garth Allen for his sharp blend of scholarly and business sense. I am grateful to both faculty members and students of the following establishments: the College of St Mark & St John, Plymouth, England, Ryerson University, Toronto, and Bentley College in Waltham, Massachussetts, together with the libraries of those same institutions, as well as the Bodleian Library, Oxford. I am grateful to those who gave me permission to quote their work. May I also apologize to any copyright-holder whom I may inadvertently have failed to contact for permission to cite their work and whose efforts I shall gladly acknowledge in any future editions of this book.

I wish to thank several practitioners for their valuable assistance, and my friends for their support and insight. I am especially grateful to Sue Wolstenholme and her family, Javed Siddiqi, Eric Austin, Stuart Smith, Ralph Sutton, Stephen Lakis, Tim Sargeant, Keith Lock-wood, Liz Thompson, Amanda Johnston, Naomi Roth, Alan Worth, Darryl Wright, Mike Paez and Anthony Da Silva.

Finally, I am indebted to Sandra den Otter for her patience and endurance throughout this project.

Simon Moore
Waltham, Massachusetts
April 1996

For my parents

If it was for me to train myself my way, there would be no mould in which I would wish to be set without being able to throw it off.

Michel de Montaigne

CHAPTER ONE

Three Moments of Communication

Shooting the dog

I began my career in public relations with a large multinational consultancy. Its larger offices are staffed by people from around the world, and its senior executives spend a lot of their time in aeroplanes. On one occasion, when the Frankfurt office was chasing an important business opportunity, it called in one of our company's top executives from his base in the United States. Finch was determined, occasionally ornery, and extremely imaginative. He worked hard and persuasively on the account, and finally visited the offices of the company whose business he was chasing. There he formally presented his proposals, accompanied by a small dog. Although his ideas were well received, his audience spent much of the meeting wondering about the dog, which sat quietly and played no obvious role in the proceedings. Finally, Finch said:

'Thank you for your time. I hope you liked what we had to say, and more than that, I hope we can do business; and by the way, if we can't do business, I intend to shoot this dog.'

As his listeners laughed politely, Finch pulled out a pistol and pointed it at the dog. The audience fell silent. An executive felt it necessary to speak up.

'Er . . . Mister Finch . . . you . . . you don't actually intend to do that, do you?'

'I shall count to three,' said Finch.

The Chief Executive stood up.

'Mister Finch, we have other consultancies to see, you know, and we cannot sign contracts in this way . . . '

'One.'

No-one spoke.

'Two.'

'You're bluffing,' someone shouted.

'Three.' Finch pulled the trigger. The gun went off, and the dog dropped dead on the spot.

A long, shocked silence followed. Finch replaced his gun, and snapped his briefcase shut. He put on his overcoat – it was a cold day.

'Thank you for your time,' he said, and clapped his hands. The dog sprang to its feet, tail wagging. It was a circus dog, hired for the day along with the gun and blank ammunition.

Finch won the account.

Talking to the fishermen

In late 1991 a land cruiser trundled into a remote lakeshore village in the Mwanza region of Tanzania. Two nurses climbed out, carrying supplies of posters and condoms and feeling extremely apprehensive about their reception. They were aware of Tanzania's serious AIDS problem (at that time most estimates agreed that three-quarters of a million citizens were HIV-positive), and that hostility to outsiders bringing news of unknown diseases had impeded United Nations efforts to control the virus. An earlier plan, co-ordinated from Europe, failed to contact the audience that mattered most – the large numbers of mobile workers who moved constantly across country and between Tanzania and Kenya, where around twenty thousand people were AIDS patients. Truckers, seasonal labourers, miners, refugee camp inhabitants and semi-nomadic fishermen were and are lacing the virus through a network of towns and villages.

A more effective initiative was urgently needed, and in 1991 several development agencies and medical foundations joined with the Tanzanian government to launch a strictly national communications programme especially aimed at high-risk areas of the country like Mwanza. A method had to be found that explained the deadly implications of AIDS to the shifting populations in the vulnerable areas and the communities they visited; and that promoted safe sex using condoms provided by a new distribution system. It was finally decided to take the messages directly into the settlements with leadership from the local people themselves: 'peer health educators' would be more likely than strangers to win the confidence of audiences in their own districts. Two people, a man and a woman, were carefully chosen from each area. They were trained, equipped with learning materials and nursing support – including the two women we left on the shore of Lake Victoria – and integrated into the general plan. Meanwhile the fishing communities learned of the planned visits from an information campaign featured on local radio. Their scattered settlements were also contacted by public health officials, mobile exhibitions, videos, and even loudspeaker messages from cross-country vehicles. Many of the teething troubles were ironed out in a pilot information campaign aimed at selected truck stops between Kenya and Tanzania. Although its launch was greeted with suspicion, the programme was gradually accepted, and then became very popular. Tanzanian Health Ministry staff, backed by the local truckers' programme, are now 'classified as VIPs' by the inhabitants.[1] Better still, enthusiastic truck drivers themselves discussed the scheme on the other side of the border. On World AIDS day in 1991, one thousand Kenyans met at the small town of Mashinari on the main highway between Mombasa and Nairobi to mark the event. Two-thirds of the town showed up, and three hundred people from surrounding villages. 'Two years ago,' it was afterwards noted, 'it is doubtful if anyone in this small community would have paid much attention to World AIDS day, despite international publicity on the subject and data showing that communities along the major trans-Africa highways are at special risk.'[2]

Clearly international publicity alone had not made the impact many hoped for, but now things had clearly changed for the better. As soon as the nurses began arranging their materials, it became obvious to them that a change in attitudes towards safe sex had finally occurred. Fishermen came running and paddling up. 'Why didn't you come sooner?' they asked.[3]

The role of trousers in modern public relations

I bought a pair of trousers at a large department store; a new line made of wrinkle-free cotton, promoted by a light-hearted video running on a loop above the display. On my way home I put my hands in the pockets, and found a thumb-sized slip of paper. It read: 'I have personally examined every detail of this garment to make sure it meets our high quality standards. Thank you for buying our product. Inspector: 16.'[4]

It takes a second to place a tiny slip in a pocket, and a second for the customer to read it. In reading the slip, the customer receives a message about the products that the garment firm makes, and is even given an identity for every product's inspector. It is a very direct, and cheap method of making an impression about the company's commitment to quality, not through a press, television or radio campaign costing tens of thousands, but through a pair of trousers. The trousers are much more effective than a newspaper article since every purchaser will inevitably read the message in the pocket – something that even the biggest, loudest, advertising and public relations campaigns could not guarantee. Someone, somewhere, had spotted a useful communications opportunity.

If a pair of trousers can play a useful part in public relations, what can't?

NOTES

1 Golden World Entry, 1991. American Medical Relief Foundation, p 5.
2 Ibid.
3 Ibid.
4 Hagar wrinkle-free cotton pants. Eatons department store, Toronto, 1994.

CHAPTER TWO

Walls of Sounds:
The Arrival of Public Relations

BEGINNINGS

Unlike human beings, an organization is no better than the impression it makes in the minds of people who know about it. That is why public relations exists. Yet once these certainties have been stated, the subject for discussion suddenly becomes tricky to pin down. It has its own customs and experts, and we tend to know it under many names: public affairs, investor relations, corporate communications, sometimes plain communications. The descriptions differ according to personal, professional or regional tastes. Yet whatever name it is known by, each act of public contact between organizations and audiences rests upon ideas and techniques still embraced by the term 'public relations'.

Nor is it certain whether public relations is a profession. Its behaviour is not constrained by the same strict procedures, rules and regulations as insurance, medicine, academics, civil engineering or even advertising. You will not need professional qualifications to practise public relations. You will not rank with such secure professional cadres as solicitors and accountants, to whom the law occasionally insists that citizens must turn. It is definitely unlike all forms of marketing, including advertising. Commercial advertising charges an expensive commission from purchasing spaces for sending messages: whether an electric space created by radio or television, or a paper space in a newspaper or a poster. Public relations is less fortunate. It cannot rely on the same straight path to profit, for it has to use as many different 'spaces' as it can find. Advertising is one route open to it; but many of the spaces public relations needs for its messages are freely available and not directly for sale – a distributed brochure, a public meeting, a letter, a sponsored event, a press release, even trousers and circus dogs. Public relations does not prosper on the purchase of these physical spaces, but on charging a fee for exploiting a visual or verbal 'space' imaginatively – often several spaces at the same time – and in the creation of messages to suit each of them. A commercial is an obvious, subjective, attempt to sell us something, but is not necessarily the ideal or the most economical way of sending a message, especially if it only needs to reach a few dozen well-

informed people. Public relations is not restricted to one medium of communication; its attraction is its skill at presenting a complex argument or making
a point in discrete settings that are harder to ignore or dismiss as bias: a
report in a newspaper, a public demonstration, a classroom education pack, a
question and answer session. There is often an element of information
exchange with audiences that cultivates the impression of a shared message,
a two-way dialogue.

For all this activity, it must be admitted that public relations is not exactly
a business, either. Communications is undeniably a commodity, and public
relations is one of the forms it takes. Telecommunications, television and
radio, are others; also politics, marketing and advertising. But public relations uses them all, technical and conceptual alike. It is certainly true that it
generates hundreds of millions of pounds, dollars and deutschmarks for
thousands of businesses around the world. It is also true that public relations
is practised by non-commercial organizations, many with strong feelings
against business: charities, theatres, campaign groups, some governments
and politicians. Public relations is just as ready to represent non-business
organizations and contact non-business audiences. Their activities widen the
breadth of commercial public relations – extending its menu of practical
methods, encouraging the cross-fertilization of creative ideas between rival
organizations, and perhaps helping us to better understand the other person's
point of view.

To worsen the task of definition further, it is easy to be subjective about
what public relations is and what it is not. Valid public relations is hard to
define and vulnerable whenever we confuse it – and we often do – with
issues that upset us. 'Some environmentalists criticize Jeep and Geo tree-
planting campaigns as being nothing more than a public relations ploy,'
reads a summary of a report on both car companies.[1] 'Any firm that looks at
ethics solely as a public relations tool to enhance its image is at ethical risk,'
warns a respected academic. 'A firm's ethical reputation is not determined
by a press release.'[2] Yes it is. Do not suppose that public relations only
equals press releases, or has nothing useful to contribute to a firm's ethical
reputation. For anybody who totally rejects an organization's position – on
ethics, the environment, and so on – it is often good enough to dismiss it as
mere 'public relations', as if 'PR's' very involvement proved a policy's actual insincerity and weakness. But of course, if the same person supports the
arguments of another organization, the public relations that it must also use
to communicate them is overlooked. It is believed to be telling the 'truth',
which rises serenely to the surface as if the way of its telling was irrelevant.
Pressure groups and big corporations may actually use similar means to
communicate, but often, in the eyes of the audience, only one of them, the
'untrue' one, is guilty of using public relations. If those rivals are fortunate,
though, the same sort of person will have been working on their respective
behalfs: someone with the experience to mix and match existing commun-

ications ideas and set them to work on new problems, or better still with the imagination to seize unexpected opportunities for communicating. These are characteristics that, in a perfect world, should define a public relations practitioner.

Public relations is a task many people feel able to handle instinctively. Often they can: the ability to communicate sophisticated individual desires is an ingrained human characteristic. But what happens if you have to communicate with a person or a group of people of whom you have never previously heard? What if the decisions they make could affect the success of your organization, even your own future? Would you choose to communicate in a way that gratifies you? Or would you be intelligent enough to find out a little about the nature of your audience – how do *they* prefer their communications? The most that can be said about this thing called public relations is that, taken as a whole, it is a service practised by and for organizations of all shapes and sizes; that it often seems to assume almost as many forms as there are problems and people; that it has expanded into a definable role, uniquely its own, during the course of the twentieth century; that it operates with a surprising amount of freedom and creativity; that it has of late experienced explosive growth and, in some areas, is the first consideration before other matters of solid policy; that it has the capacity to make a lasting impression by tapping the power of communications; and that, lastly, it springs from the natural and ancient desire to communicate, especially among human-made organizations that are growing in the complexity and range of their relationships with other organizations or individuals.

Perhaps surprisingly for something that sprang from such a fundamental human instinct, it was only recently that communications threw itself out along the branch that we call public relations. Still more surprisingly, the conditions that made public relations possible were unwittingly identified three centuries ago in two satirical sentences in *Tale of a Tub*: 'Whoever hath an ambition to be heard in a crowd,' wrote Jonathan Swift, 'must press, and squeeze, and thrust, and climb with indefatigable pains, till he has exalted himself to a certain degree of altitude above them.' Here are the perpetual obstacles to effective communications: noise and competition. If the first sentence explains the situation, Swift's second sentence presents the problem that public-relations people spend their working lives struggling to solve. 'Now, in all assemblies, though you wedge them ever so close, we may observe this peculiar property, that over their heads there is room enough, but how to reach it is the difficult point; it being as hard to get quit of number, as of hell.'[3] Swift's prose mixes elegance with brutality, and communicators should explore as many unexpected sources as possible for a suitable argument or image. Now there is much more here than a venerable fragment of soothsaying and a sarcastic (if accurate) description of the need that drives public relations. Swift, to be sure, had no conception of the future existence of public relations. His relevance to us is tangential, but noteworthy, because he noticed the coming, revolutionary, conjunction of the two forces that caused public relations to develop and to profoundly influence our lives. For in Swift's time, the opportunities for people to communicate began accelerating, pricked, as public relations still is, by the expanding demands of trade and industry, of markets at home and abroad, of movement between the social classes, of a broader and steadily opening political structure. Naturally, this turbulence radically increased contact between new organizations and new audiences, motivated by the growth of commerce and needing each other's custom or support for fame and fortune, or simply for survival. On the other side, the tricky fact was – as it still is – that the growth in people with things to say made it more difficult for anyone to be heard.

Several writers and historians have identified one effect of this conjunction: the outbreak of massive 'publicity battles' in the early nineteenth century that would be recognizable to us today. In Britain, the Prince Regent and his estranged wife used the press, politicians and public opinion to support their arguments. In the United States, the Jackson presidency retained a senior adviser who helped guide the administration's communications. 'Public opinion was the great new fact of the dawning modern world,'[4] Paul Johnson has concluded. The best way to sway public opinion is through publicity and persuasion. Centuries of scattered communications slowly assumed a distinct shape. A recognizable process emerged to deal with this surge in information. It was helped enormously by audiences and organizations finding that once they had opened the spigot, the swelling flow of messages could not be shut off easily.

In these circumstances, the arrival of specialists claiming that with their help and imagination you could be heard by the people who mattered to you, was simply a matter of time. Sure enough, the first full-time specialists appeared around the turn of the twentieth century, and called themselves publicists. Much of what they did then is still done now. Today, specialists of varying abilities concentrate their expertise in many different areas of public relations activity: from selling beans to electing politicians. They earn their livings as communicators – a vital difference, as far as public relations is concerned, between the twentieth century and earlier times. Other main differences between then and now are the higher number of tasks and audiences, and the bewildering options now available for creating and sending messages. As we shall see, this technology is changing the sort of people we are, and because of that will propel public relations into unique forms of expression. Modern communications can be instantly delivered, short-lived and swiftly forgotten, so public relations must also be decidedly forward-looking. It must constantly add to its arsenal of techniques to remain useful. It must be alert, for its own sake and on behalf of those it represents, to changes in the expectations and attitudes of society.

Public relations must therefore keep abreast of the remarkable revolution in communications technology. Its best practitioners must be able to identify in advance new tools to use at the moment their audiences look ready to appreciate them. They must be equally ready to discard trusted and familiar techniques. In a short time, the video has become a commonplace method of communication – video news releases, video news services to employees, annual reports put on video and distributed worldwide. Videos will soon be unoriginal, mined to the point of exhaustion. Newer machines await us. Executives may one day be able to transmit live, holographic images of distant participants into a real-life conference chamber. In Britain, a major newspaper publisher is developing a portable electronic 'newspaper'. The light, book-sized box is designed for rail commuters, who will be able to mark and save useful articles. It is recharged overnight, when next day's content is transmitted. News releases flit across the Internet: the crude beginnings of a revolution, perhaps a perpetual revolution, in the way public relations will communicate.

The fact is that change can hardly fail to affect public relations and its audiences. At the very least, there is an attractive novelty in change. And do not underrate novelty: it is vital to public relations, because it is unexpected it can have a vigorous impact. The prospect of fresh equipment in the future, and the need to understand and monitor social attitudes if communications is to strike a chord with its intended public, obliges good public relations to remain perpetually flexible and alert to 'future shock'. This book suggests ways that coming technology will affect our view of ourselves, of information, and the character of the organizations wrapping that information into public relations.

As in all fields of endeavour, the wider the exposure to experience and ideas, the better the resulting work. Public relations cannot become too self-absorbed in order to remain effective; nor should it devote much attention to wrapping itself in trappings of professional exclusivity. For the moment, public-relations researchers and practitioners may roam freely over other subjects to enrich their own work. Communications is the inheritance of us all, and the study of closely structured communications initiatives – for that is public relations – should embrace the broadest possibilities of human experience.

Public relations must be as intensely engaged with the present as with the future. It has to work with the ideas and perceptions of people as they stand revealed at any moment. It is swept along by audience perceptions and because of this can, at its best, express a pure and exciting originality denied to traditional business activities. That is why there are in these pages many accounts of modern public relations at work. The story of a communications problem is as interesting to tell as any other sort of story. It is an effective way of making a point about the creation of public relations ideas, about the potential for imagination, and about the distillation of the communications process into, ideally, a taut, disciplined, strategy speeding an organization forward to its intended goal.

Unfortunately, public relations spares little time for looking over its shoulder to see what it can learn from the past. The past can appear threatening to communicators who rely on their ability to pledge fresh ideas. Technology aside, a good deal of their bag of tricks contains old wisdom half-remembered or repackaged. We all strive for originality but we are, more often than might be supposed, merely restating in ways appropriate to our age and experience much of what has already been experienced or conceived long before. Too often, we do not take proper advantage of the cold fact that the foundation of the latest 'new' idea was bequeathed to us by others, long dead and forgotten. Public relations, fast-moving, regenerative and prosperous, would benefit from closer scrutiny of the past. It can, if it chooses, draw upon several thousand years of interesting case studies to justify its existence: there are many ancient schemes from which it can profit.

It has already been observed that the wish to communicate with one another is as old as our species – the desire of one individual or group to have relations with other large groups of people certainly pre-dates Jonathan Swift. It is closely linked to the prehistoric organization of roaming bands into clans, or into farming and trade settlements under leaders, and with the beginnings of an organized religion. At that point, communities or organizations began investing some thought into the sorts of messages they needed to send to others: perhaps to traders, nearby settlements, devotees of the first organized cults, the gods themselves, the dead, the earth, men and women. Humanity, it seems, has often felt a need to set aside spontaneous commun-ications, to carefully arrange problems into messages, and to direct them at audiences in a vivid way. The earliest specialists – kings, chiefs, priests, traders – took roughly the same approach as the most up-to-date consultant. We can trace the beginnings of public relations to the first man who, twenty thousand years ago, wriggled on his belly along a rock tunnel some forty or fifty yards long, deep inside a cavern near what is now Lascaux in southern France. At the end of the tunnel he found himself in an enormous hall of rock, now known as Trois Frères. There, he and later unrecorded generations chose to create Europe's oldest works of art: mammoth, horse, deer, fish, some spurting blood from imaginary wounds. Above them all hovers the 'Sorcerer', the staring face and beard of a part man, part beast. It is a phantasmic, dancing figure communicated to us by our most distant ancestors.[5]

What does it mean? For whom were the images at Lascaux prepared, or their stunning counterparts at Altamira or Pech-Merle, and those most recently discovered at the Sormiou calanque? Systematic attempts to understand our ultimate past are usually preserved for archaeologists or anthropologists, but on this occasion the underpinnings of public relations have a little to contribute. It once seemed easy to explain the paintings as a whimsy, a random impulse, a primal urge for self-expression. But, as anyone engaged in public relations knows, the message cannot be divorced from its setting. The setting at Lascaux deserves our attention because, without it, those paintings would indeed be no more than beautiful daubs, self-centred acts of individual creativity. But the Trois Frères pictures were only made once their creators decided on the setting. The artist (or artists) wriggled through a stony and frighteningly low tube, in places no higher than their shoulder blades. Only after a good deal of bumping, bruising, and incipient claustrophobia were they at last able to stand, and create. 'One thing is clear,' ventured E. H. Gombrich, 'no one would have crawled so far into the eerie depth of the earth simply to decorate such an inaccessible place.'[6] What made that chamber so special that, in spite of the endurance required to reach it, there and there only could the images be made? The chamber itself must have meant a great deal to the image-makers. It was special, and in placing their images in that place, the painters were sending a distinct message. Trois Frères is obviously not the product of a casual urge to paint; it lies at the end of a carefully thought out communication strategy directed at an audience likely to be influenced, then as now, by two influences: the way the message is delivered – here conveyed in animal images that we are unlikely ever to decode completely; and the means of delivery – in this case a vast subterranean cavern connected to the upper world by a hollow creeping thread, fastened into rock.

A thread of ascent also connects Trois Frères to the computers that will soon react not only to our voices, but to gestures or looks. Perhaps few ideas, few means of delivering messages have become so outmoded as to be wholly useless. The force of the visual image is, for instance, as important to us today as it was when the first person struggled into the cavern at Lascaux to paint those startling, vital, forms. The power of animal representation is still much respected in communications – as Jaguar or Panda owners, busy pumping tigers into their tanks, would doubtless agree. It is also revealed in the impressions conjured up when associating Britons with bulldogs or lions, the Russians with bears or the Chinese with dragons.

Communications is free, an opportunity and a skill granted to all human beings at birth. Our excitable cells, charged with electric impulses, assist our brains to fuse pictures, metaphors, principles and other ideas into our minds according to the world we individually see about us. We have an existence independent of robotic instinct. We express this existence to each other through the medium of communications with, and between, the organizations we have built to minister to or restrain ourselves. As organizations become more complicated and more invasive, so too do the ways we see Communication. It slowly acquires characteristics of its own, a limited terminology of its own, a technological tool-kit, experts skilled in certain types of expression and new audiences. It becomes public relations.

THE BOOK

An 'invitation' is not the same as an 'introduction'. Introductions are only made *after* we have chosen to meet another person or a new field. In an introduction, we mentally make a methodical map of the new person or field's main features, find out a little about their background and if necessary ask for references to enable us to continue our exploration in more detail. Fortunately, several excellent introductions to public relations are already available, and some of these appear in a bibliography at the end of this book. Introductions, to repeat, only occur after the original decision to meet has been taken. But what, ideally, would motivate us to make that original decision? Surely the best invitations to meet any subject, human or intellectual, are the ones that convey fascination and curiosity. We have been intrigued by what we have heard in advance, excited by the words and pictures conjured up in our minds. The design and wording of the invitation card itself may hint at the richness of the encounter. This book invites you to consider making that encounter. It depicts an area of work and thought that can offer ample scope for the imagination. It will demonstrate that public relations has a long and traceable lineage. From an erratic, but clearly discernible sequence of historical precedents, the structuring of communications initiatives into intricate programmes has endowed public relations with a life, purpose and vitality of its own.

Nowadays, all sorts of matters, from increasing productivity to the enforcement of Government policy, are regarded as communications problems. The plans of businesses, politics and voluntary groups are organized around communications. Good communicators comb the world for new ideas. They employ their own researchers and publications, run their own consultancies and departments, manage their own budgets. They are investigating new ways of reaching increasingly knowledgeable and influential audiences. They build sophisticated programmes for delivering simple messages on behalf of other people. Public relations is now being studied as a branch of business and the social sciences. There is as much to study as there are ways to communicate; there are as many organizations that wish to communicate as there are audiences for their messages.

This book will try to explain what to expect from public relations as a practitioner or as an audience. It briefly sets out the tools, and critically surveys the manner in which those tools are used and abused. Above all, it shows that flexible, creative, and busy minds can pick their way through an increasingly complex mesh of communications, and enrich the working lives of other communicators, and perhaps of society generally. Public relations *is* now a discipline of sorts. At any rate, it is no longer a cipher, the willing slave of such organizations as occasionally condescend to notice it. In some areas it is becoming the master.

It is important to make clear how public relations actually works, and to offer an impression of the various forms it takes. Many of its pioneers had backgrounds in journalism and business. A number of them are responsible for identifying those basic truths that govern the field. Following in their wake are present-day practitioners and academics who conduct minute investigations into the remotest reaches of existing public relations. All this is necessary and significant.[7] Certainly, exposure to the fullest scope of communications fills a communicator's working life with options and reduces pressure. I also believe, in this regard, that an act as comprehensive as communications must take the trouble to embrace as many other experiences as it can, to broaden rather than to narrowly concentrate. This book surveys some of the possibilities of that wider world. Few attempts at communicating are too small, old, or advanced for public relations experts to explore for ideas. I was reminded of this on the same day that I received from my editor some reflections on the first draft of this manuscript. In the *New York Times* that lay on my desk beside his letter, France Telecom had placed a full-page advertisement: '20,000 years ago we were on the cutting edge of technology. And we've been there ever since.' Above the text was the image of a running aurochs (wild cow) taken from the cavern at Trois Frères, along with a perceptive caption: 'Some of the earliest attempts to communicate abstract ideas can be found at the Lascaux caves in the Dordogne region of France.'[8] Well, the confirmation of one's grand speculations by sudden evidence that those ideas are not the least bit original is more common than is usually admitted, as is the odd blend of satisfaction and chagrin that such moments produce.

Your invitation, then, is a blend of description, argument and speculation. We have noted that public relations is about pre-meditated communications, about the task of carefully structuring a message and sending it in an appealing way to a pre-selected audience. It is not always easy to impose order on this process, but most organizations now believe that there is a need to do so. It is therefore important to survey public relations at work, which is why the next chapter concerns shameless hype. The production of physical and verbal spectacle, designed to make an impact on as many people as possible, allows the fundamentals of public relations to spring from the page in a brash and entertaining way. Chapter four examines the two human forces engaged in public relations – the communicating organization and the message-receiving (and then often responding) audience. These two groups must exist in order that public relations might exist. The fifth chapter is a polemic: even the most blatant forms of public relations rely on originality and flexibility in expression and ideas, and the recruitment of imaginative people. Of its many branches of activity, issues management must often be as subtle, understated and sensitive as the hype for a new product should be colourful and attention-grabbing. The subject of two chapters, it tackles delicate problems that impede, often stop and even ruin, a careless organization carrying out its regular tasks – from local: the arrival of a large, dirty production site in a small, rural community; to international: the activities of a corporation in a country with a dubious human rights record. Public relations practitioners are commonly recruited to handle such matters.

From issues management, the text turns to explore the arrangement made between public relations and the holders of power, who have always recognized that effective communications can consolidate or expand their authority. What would-be leaders have too often ignored is the hold communications has over them, reducing some, more frequently of late, to total dependence or near-subservience. Three chapters are devoted to a discussion of the place of honesty and moral rectitude in public relations. It is a vital issue: the communication of untruth has perpetuated human misery and incited people to cruelty. Two of these chapters balance conceptions of truth and evil in communications, and the last ponders the effect of global communications on the relation between audiences and organizations. We see that public relations liberates when organizations need to attract support from a well-informed audience. Access to alternative information equips that audience with choice, and increases its power over the communicators, who must make extra efforts to put their messages across. As the audience becomes more flexible and less habitual, the available communications options must be refined. Organizations with something to say must spend a lot of time on public relations, seeking ways to stand out from the 'noise' generated by the sheer volume of information already on offer, and to tackle arguments put about by competitors or opponents. The need to persuade, and not just inform, becomes more important; successful persuasion needs dialogue; dialogue equalizes influence. In this way public relations can work as a liberating force.

Finally, as we advance into yet another great social change, engineered by communications technology, a closing section speculates on the new public relations that the next generation of practitioners can look forward to developing.

NOTES

1 Infotrac. National Newspaper Index. Citation of report 'Honk if you love the environment', *Los Angeles Times*, 23 March 1991, p D1
2 Cooke, Robert Allan. 'Danger signs of unethical behaviour: how to determine if your firm is at ethical risk, *Journal of Business Ethics*, 10: 1991, pp 249–53. I am grateful to Professor Cooke for drawing my attention to the work of Ludwig von Mises.
3 Swift, Jonathan. *Tale of a Tub*. From *Gulliver's Travels and Other Writings* (Boston: Houghton Mifflin, 1960. First published in 1704) p 271.
4 Johnson, Paul. *The Birth of the Modern* (London: Phoenix, 1992) p 530.
5 Grigson, Geoffrey. *The Painted Caves* (London: Phoenix, 1957) pp 138–9; Campbell, Joseph. *Primitive Mythology: The Masks of God* (London: Penguin, rev. ed. 1976) pp 309–10.
6 Gombrich, E H. *The Story of Art* (Oxford: Phaidon, 15th edition, 1989) p 22.
7 A bibliography is attached.
8 *New York Times*, 29 September 1994, p D7.

CHAPTER THREE

Up Front and In Your Face

'I wondered which single factor has most transformed the British scene, and now I have little doubt: it is publicity.'[1] This comment by Anthony Sampson, an eminent observer of modern trends, applies to the western scene in general, and is true of emerging economies elsewhere. Publicity, the business of getting media coverage, numbers among the oldest and the most boisterous of public relation's offspring. It is what most people think of when asked to define public relations. At its least subtle, publicity resorts to hype. There can be no other way of introducing public relations to the overly-shy or the curious.

WYNY/FM Radio, New York. 25 June 1990. 6.30 and 7pm. News previews:

Newscaster: Coming up in thirty minutes, ever wonder what happens to the holes in Life Saver candy?

D.J.: How did you know it was on the tip of my tongue this morning?

Newscaster: Are you ready for Life Saver Holes? A one-calorie candy from Life Savers will be making its debut in November. And just think how many they've had all these years.

WNSR/R Radio, New York. 25 June 1990. 5.55pm. The News:

Debbie Gross: Jim Douglas has been excited about this one all day because he's had a hard time sleeping nights ever since he was a kid just wondering what they do with those little holes from Life Savers. Well, now thanks to the folks who make the candy, he will be able to get some shut-eye. The candy company is coming out with Life Saver holes in all of your favorite flavors. It promises those little chunks will fit perfectly into the middle of a regular Life Saver.

Jim Douglas (D.J.): I'll sure have to buy all the Life Savers I can now and match the colors.

Why on earth is this news? How did the launch of a 'bite-size' sweet make the pages of *Time* magazine, not to mention *Newsweek* and *CNN*? Is it really important, or a lot of hype? Is it even useful to distinguish between the two?

Hype, hyperbole, exaggeration, puffery, something not intended to be taken literally. The term changes with the generations, but it is often found at the root of scepticism towards public relations. The two have come to mean publicity at all costs, damaging truth and preventing alternative coverage of useful news. Hype is noisy, colourful, gate-crashing. Hype is distracting and absurd. Hype is stunts and celebrities. Hype is the circus coming to town. A new sweet would emphatically not have made national news coverage, even in America, if Life Savers had relied solely on advertisement hoardings and television commercials. Holes became news because public relations experts employed hype to give a strictly commercial message a story, an attractive 'hook' on which media articles could be hung. The brighter, more escapist and apparently sillier the product, the more promising the prospect for hype.

There is a strong bond between hype and a certain type of public relations. It is inevitable that this sort of public relations is the sort that people remember; it is noisy and visible and it has to be. It is the polar opposite of public affairs – although the invisibility of public affairs communications has provoked similar concerns about extent and influence. Hype is different. You know exactly were you stand with it, say cynics: on the verge of mindless entertainment or halfway up the garden path to a lie. Hype, in the minds of some people, is the publicist Max Clifford promoting clients via the sexual organs of British cabinet ministers. It is largely remembered through its triviality or its misdeeds, as depicted in the popular press. The press and hype often need each other. The press gorges on hype to fatten its pages; hype needs the press to publicize its activities on behalf of people, events or organizations. Hype aggressively goes after 'ink', after coverage. Unlike some other forms of public relations, it depends heavily on the media. Hype is a serious business. It is the tough business of delivering something that may employ thousands of people and consume millions of pounds in research development. Through the media it is reaching people with a set of standard messages that they are able to act on: buy this, visit that, celebrate this, cheer that.

In the 1870s, John Philip Holland, a British subject, Irish nationalist and US citizen, used hype to gain American government funding for his struggle to construct the first workable submarine. He wrote and published a dramatic article entitled 'Can New York be Bombarded?' Fear of foreign attack on US harbours was already widespread, and the sensation provoked by Holland's article produced an immediate public response from the American Navy. It offered funds for the presentation of an effective submarine design. Holland won the competition, with a design that formed the prototype for all submarines up to the end of World War II. It is a suggestive point of ethics: Holland played on public concern about military attack to help him develop a formidable weapon of war – which, incidentally, increased the likelihood of the very attack he encouraged people to worry about. He forced a response from his most important audience, the Navy, and took advantage of it. His publicity was employed to intensify fear, and the construction of a war machine that was later one of the biggest threats to American and Allied victory in two world wars.

Americans were chief among the early hypesters; their press agents were responsible for whipping up popular publicity as often and as volubly as they could on behalf of their clients. The depth to which hype had penetrated people's minds as early as the turn of the century is demonstrated in the diaries of Robert Peary. He claimed in 1909 to be the first man to reach the North Pole, and without any firm supporting evidence but with a talent for public relations got the rest of the world to believe in what was in all probability a lie. Peary's understanding of public relations was masterful. In fact, it might with justice be said that he demonstrated the dark side of its power – to subvert the truth. Nevertheless, it should be admitted that the methods Peary employed were imaginative. His rival, Doctor Frederick Cook, was sitting at a banquet in Copenhagen arranged by journalists to celebrate his own, also fabricated, claim to have reached the North Pole. Peary was still far away in the Arctic, but his press agents were planning a publicity stunt of their own:

> Suddenly attendants appeared carrying sheafs of cables, which were placed under the plates of all the journalists in the room. Cook received one too. As he opened it, he sensed a lull falling over the assembly. William Stead, the senior journalist present, stood up and read his copy. It contained a single, blunt sentence: 'In a wire from Indian Harbor, Labrador, dated September 6, 1909, Peary says: Stars and Stripes nailed to the pole.'
>
> Cook's expression gave no hint of any inner turbulence as he rose to his feet to congratulate Peary. 'There is glory enough for us all,' he declared; and at that the affair broke up as the journalists rushed off to duty.[2]

Peary and Cook fought a lengthy battle in the American newspapers, supported by still-familiar public-relations initiatives: lectures, publications, sponsorships, the formation of clubs of supporters, public support from respected independent experts (now known as 'third-party endorsement'). Peary emerged victorious because his talent for publicity was much more acute. The man's excellent sense of self-promotion would win admiration from present-day practitioners of public relations. As he returned from Greenland by ship, sick and debilitated from his remarkable journey, Peary feverishly filled his diary with plans to secure his claim and his fame:

March 26: Have my eye glasses mounted gold for constant use. Have extra pair ditto as a present to someone . . .

March 28: . . . piece of North Pole bearskin fringe for souvenirs to women. The North Pole flag with white bar. This as a stamp on all North Pole articles?

April 5: North Pole coats, suits, tents, cookers at Sportsmens Show with male & female attendants in Eskimo costume . . . portrait of me in deer or sheep coat with bear roll (face unshaven), . . . Have Foster color in a special print of this to bring out the gray eyes, the red sunburned skin, the bleached eyebrows and beard, frosted eyebrows, eye glasses, beard.

April 6: Have Harpers take entire matter, book, magazine articles, pictures and stories ($100,000).

April 9: . . . send photo President & self shaking hands to him . . . send Roosevelt a Pole Peary sledge.[3]

Then, as now, the media slavered over the entertainment value inherent in hype. It was entertainment, but it also managed to be news – a promise peculiar to this form of public relations. Hype took nothing seriously except itself, and because of this mushroomed into a way of winning good publicity for any valuable product dependent upon public support. Hollywood, whose business was obviously dependent on massive public patronage, turned to hype to promote its movies and its actors. '*I* named her,' an ageing, neglected, publicist complains of a studio star in Evelyn Waugh's sharp and funny Hollywood novel *The Loved One*, '*I* made her an antifascist refugee. *I* said she hated men because of her treatment by Franco's Moors. That was a new angle then. It caught on.'[4] It certainly did. In 1925 the mogul Samuel Goldwyn produced *Dark Angel*, featuring his newest star, the beautiful Hungarian Vilma Banky. Her co-star was Rudolph Valentino, who developed a strong personal interest in Miss Banky. 'This', Goldwyn's biographer observes, 'was a publicity break better than any Goldwyn could have imagined.' He immediately engaged Ray Coffin, a publicity director. A month before the picture's debut, Coffin faked a story about a Hungarian Baron who had proposed to Banky and was desperate to win her back. This fiction attracted so much coverage that Coffin even held a full-blown press conference, hiring a European actor to play the part of the non-existent Budapest Baron. Valentino, complained the 'Baron':

Plays with my darling and is famous for his attractiveness. Is my darling under his spell? Or is Goldwyn bribing her with an immense salary in order to keep her loveliness for his pictures and away from me?[5]

Such shenanigans are still fairly common public-relations stuff, allowing for the more intimate tastes of today's tabloids. In 1925, they had a tremendous impact. 'Overnight, the Hungarian actress would be installed in the world's most royal order – movie star.'[6]

Shortly after Peary's polar public relations, a candy-maker from Cleveland realized that hard mints could cope with the sweltering Ohio summer more successfully than chocolate. Clarence Crane wanted to set his new product apart from the small square competition sold in Europe, so in 1912 he made his mints circular and punched a hole through the middle. They looked like tiny versions of the life preservers used at sea, so Crane called them Life Savers. After a few years, his product was purchased by a New York advertising executive, and became extremely popular. Life Savers expanded, passed through several purchases and diversified into new flavours which have since become a minor American tradition, the biggest selling hard candies and sugarless mints in the country. In 1990 Planters Life Savers developed 'Holes', the mythical missing centres from Life Savers and, the manufacturers hoped, the launch of a new American tradition. There was simply no way of awakening consumers to what one executive described as 'a fun, new way to enjoy Life Savers' by treating 'Holes' with gravity, so hype was liberally employed. Burson-Marsteller, the public relations consultancy retained for the launch, agreed with the need to 'focus on the "fun"',[7] and decided to construct a gigantic pun on the product's name. 'Put Holes in your pockets' urged the message on several of the complementary accessories designed for the product's launch, which was held in 'Pockets', a cafe and billiards establishment in New York City. The media invitations resembled a mini-pool table, with the product emerging from each of the pockets. 'You're invited to get the HOLES story', it declared, announcing the birth of the 'first bite-size candy to come in fruit flavors', and billing – as an added attraction – a trick shot show by America's number one women's billiards champion. Fifty media attended, and were treated to pizza pocket sandwiches. This two-hour mix of fairground and hard business was capped by a short, twenty-minute presentation on the product, publicity literature and a large cake shaped like a Life Saver with its hole full of Holes. Possibly tasteless, garish certainly, but the most likely way to draw the attention of the media towards mere sweets. For those failing to attend, film footage of the Holes story, the manufacturing process and the commercials was distributed along with the press kit and sample products. The public-relations team exploited the national affection for Life Savers, and decided to 'incorporate Life Savers heritage in all communications'[8] by preparing background releases on the product's long history.

The headline coverage reflected the hype: 'Life Saver's tasty holes', 'Life Saver getting hole-some', 'Marketing the middle'. The whole project is a good example of marketing public relations, and the value of putting traditional communications tools like launch events and news releases at the service of an original message. A Life Savers news bureau was established, contacting media with story ideas in advance of the national appearance of the product: profit forecasts, recipes ('Fruity popcorn balls', 'mint chocolate chews'). Prepared stories ('Put Holes in your Christmas stocking'), set out in the form of a completed news article, were distributed to attract small local newspapers interested in saving money on the cost of preparing articles for print. A 'cause-related' opportunity was also identified with the 'Hole in the Wall Gang Camp', established by the actor Paul Newman for children with cancer or potentially fatal blood diseases. Planters Life Savers Holes helped Hole in the Wall fund a new nature centre. In this case the commitment was considered more important than the immediate publicity, which was restricted to a news release and photograph when the cheque was presented.

It is easy to feel frustrated, possibly repelled, by the razzmatazz of hype, and to ignore the careful planning that must underpin it. As with any other public-relations project, ideas are delivered to audiences only after careful advance planning and constant monitoring of progress. Campaigns aiming to generate as much publicity as possible do not always have to be as exclusive about their target audiences as more self-important forms of public relations like financial relations or issues management. In this case Burson-Marsteller only identified two main publics, men and women over eighteen, and children. Adults absorbed the heritage message, kids got the bad jokes. Hype could not exist without print and broadcast media, and the team concentrated on reaching their consumers through national magazines, major newspapers, the 'suburban' or local newspapers, television and radio. The trade media also mattered in order to encourage grocery and convenience stores, drug stores, mass merchandizers, candy and tobacco wholesalers to stock up their shelves.

The Holes campaign illustrates the advantages of using intensive publicity. In Life Saver's successful marketing campaign public relations worked in close co-operation with advertising. A massive ad campaign was prepared. Television commercials began as early as the end of 1989, seven months ahead of the launch, with nineteen commercials a week. A series of consumer promotions was inaugurated 'to generate awareness and trial' and encourage retailers to stock the product. One crucial and enduring difference existed between Holes' public relations and advertising activities: possibly, it is the most telling argument for any organization considering the use of public relations. Holes promised interested retailers '8-week heavy up TV advertising at a $33 million national annual rate starting 1/02/90'.[9] The public-relations budget recommendations were less than half a per cent of that figure. Public relations is highly labour-intensive. It requires a great deal of co-ordination and team-work over a range of projects. But, it remains low-cost in comparison with the sums needed to buy advertising space. The work of the Holes news bureau, the recipes, the launch itself put Holes stories all over the North American media, a final total of 88,128,363 potential readers, viewers and listeners. The total is impressive, if difficult to make detailed sense of, for how many people actually read, absorbed and acted on the necessary messages? Accurate evaluation is a difficult business that has dogged and unnecessarily diverted the public-relations industry. In this case, though, the basic figure is so large that sheer weight of numbers would seem to guarantee a large amount of message contact. The media had found the hype irresistible. 'After all,' argued Burson-Marsteller, 'the age-old mystery of "what happens to the holes?" had finally been solved.'[10] Hype is about not being serious, and that is precisely its attraction. We do not want to be serious all the time, so public relations is sensible enough to oblige us.

But who are 'We'? And who are 'They'?

NOTES

1 Sampson, Anthony. 'The anatomy of publicity'. Spectator, 7 November 1992.
2 Berton, Pierre. *The Arctic Grail* (London: Penguin, 1989) pp 601–2.
3 Ibid., pp 583–4.
4 Waugh, Evelyn. *The Loved One* (London: Chapman & Hall, 1965. First published 1948) p 12.
5 Berg, A. Scott. *Goldwyn* (New York: Knopf, 1989) p 150.
6 Ibid., p 151.
7 IPRA Golden World Entry, 1990. Marketing Communications. New Products, 'Burson-Marsteller. Life Savers Holes – Put Holes in your pockets'.
8 Ibid., 'Preliminary Public Relations Recommendations'. p 3.
9 Ibid., 'Life Savers Holes support information brochure for trade. *c.* 1989'.
10 Ibid., 'Evaluation'.

CHAPTER FOUR

Us, and Them

He refuses to be alone. He is the man of the crowd.
It will be in vain to follow; for I shall learn no more of him,
Nor of his deeds.[1]

Edgar Allen Poe

THE BUILDING BLOCKS

In public relations, there are those who give, and those who receive. The givers are generally organizations with something to communicate, either internally to their own members or to external audiences. A new superstore has to attract shoppers; a football club needs to maintain commitment from its team and loyalty from its fans; a vehicle manufacturer must introduce a special offer to its dealers; a hospital must raise funds from the local community for a new ward.

These are all different sorts of audiences, all specific publics. They are not the 'general' public. If clients talk vaguely about contacting the 'general public', answer that it does not exist in any useful way. It is comprised of separate groups affecting the course of any given communications campaign. When bankers refer to 'the general public' they might mean small investors. When sports personalities make the same remark, they are really talking about the people who take an interest in their particular sport. The non-existence of the general public is particularly important to remember here, because public relations relies so much on carefully identifying those audiences that 'own' or shape specific problems. Every time you, the audience, open your newspaper, read a brochure or watch television, you are being offered a menu of choices adapted to your taste, commitment or prejudices, but with a neutral core: described by the novelist George Orwell as 'this common basis of agreement, with its implication that human beings are all one species of animal.'[2] In this way you are identified not as a 'general', but as a 'key public' – probably as a dozen key publics – a person whose views and activities matter to certain organizations. You are hardly ever reached by information just for the sake of it. The neutral core rarely reaches us in such a 'pure' form, liberated from bias or another person's interpretation (or, if you prefer, 'spin'). If it did, it would bore you to death. It would be random, disjointed, meaningless; a mass of facts or unconnected narrative.

A story or a problem must exist for information to be refined and made useful – and usable. A value attaches to information once it is used by a person or organization with something to say about it. Whenever someone goes to the trouble of arranging information in an eye-catching way, and then sends it to you along a carefully chosen route, it is because they want you to believe their message. You are being exposed to them. Your existing purchasing prejudices are being reinforced: you may, for example, feel loyal to a particular brand of margarine because you are constantly reminded by published medical reports that it cuts cholesterol. But you are not merely being reached as a consumer, you are constantly receiving messages about practically every aspect of your life – as pedestrian, as driver, as tourist, as guest, as host, as environmentalist, as polluter, as member of a particular generation. The preparation and distribution of those messages to you is the work of public relations. Professional or amateur communicators are sending messages that encourage you to think or act in a desired way. Many opposing organizations are active in this area, from anti-industry pressure groups to multinational chemical giants. Naturally, the messages they send and the ways they communicate differ radically. A pressure group can rely on the passion and commitment of unpaid volunteers. A natural gas corporation with plans to construct a pipeline is unlikely to persuade even sympathetic local residents to demonstrate on its behalf. It must rely on different methods to make its position known, but communicate it must.

Public relations exists to help an organization achieve its goals, by ensuring that the right public thinks the right things. On many occasions, organizations, such as chemical companies and neighbourhood committees where chemical plants are sited, communicate competing ideas. They are motivated by the fact that audiences, although open to messages, are not automatically obedient to them, prepared to swallow anything public relations practitioners throw out. A modern audience, while one person or one million persons, is a sophisticated beast capable of choosing from a much wider array of messages than its parents or grandparents could. It works in an elementary fashion when the 'audience' is a dog-lover: why this brand of pet food, rather than the other thirty or so? Why buy groceries in this store, rather than one of the other four in the neighbourhood? Decision-making becomes more complicated when the audience is asked to change its attitude to an idea: that passive smoking is unhealthy, for instance, or that clear-cutting harms the environment. Since communications problems vary so much, public relations comes in all shapes and sizes. It is made to measure for each problem. The public-relations work for the annual Oxford–Cambridge boat race, is centred around a single event lasting around twenty minutes; on the other hand, a continual communications effort rolling out along yearly plans is needed by plastic-packaging companies and their opponents to influence the course of waste-recycling legislation.

To function effectively in societies receiving myriad messages and making myriad choices, public relations needs the existence of four conditions. It needs an audience to contact. It needs an organization that must contact them. It needs a message with which to make contact. It needs to divine a suitable way of sending the message. These are the building blocks of public relations, which, to be effective, must be set in place. What would you do if you had to tell a kind friend, about to return from a holiday abroad, that the clutch on her car gave out while you were driving it? You might mutter to me: 'I would tell her: "I've broken the clutch on your car. Sorry."' That, undoubtedly, is the information. Is it the exact form of words you will use? Or will you need to put it in a different way, possibly bedded in among more positive sentences? When will you say it? Will they be the first words to fall from your lips when you meet her? Even if you are the most insensitive friend in the world, you will probably want to break the news in a way that would preserve your friendship, and minimize a confrontation. Automatically, you have become 'the organization' that needs to send a message, and you begin, equally automatically and in a modest fashion, to toy with the four building blocks of carefully structured communication.

You might start with audience analysis. You have had a chance to research your friend thoroughly over the years. She may be generous with her time and possessions, but a mite irritable and stressed when confronted with bad news. Or, she may be such a nice person that you feel relaxed about telling her – or maybe guiltier. So what, exactly, do you plan to say? In these circumstances, a good grasp of key messages is important. The key message is not the basic information or the exact form of words you will use, but the idea you want to plant forever in the mind of your audience. For example defensiveness ('look, it's an old car anyway; about to break down any second'), reassurance ('I am paying a garage to fix the clutch even as we speak'), humanity ('I am sorry it happened – I hate to let a friend down like this'), maybe guilt ('luckily it broke when I was in slow traffic. I hate to think what could have happened if I'd been on the motorway . . . when was it last serviced?'). To outsiders, public relations appears to work backwards since its starting point is an identification of the ideal outcome. Once the key messages most likely to achieve that outcome have been decided, it remains to present them in a way that you think your friend, the 'audience', will appreciate. Possibly by making a telephone call to her the day before she is due to return, to give her time to get over her frustration with you; or a meeting at the airport with flowers and an apologetic smile; or a welcome home dinner. How you do it depends on the knowledge of your friend, the messages you need to deliver, and your own creativity.

Public relations takes the same elements but writes them exceeding large. Your audience is no longer a single person, but a government, consumers, a neighbourhood, a citizens' rights group. Your messages no longer relate to a faulty clutch, but maybe to contaminated food, or the impact of a new drug. You are no longer 'the organization'. Instead, you are helping to communicate on behalf of a corporation, a green group, a charity, a university. One factor stays the same: the effectiveness of your communications depends on your creativity.

US, THE AUDIENCE

Audiences are as varied in type as they are in size. A charity, for instance, communicates with its employees, its volunteers and trustees, the people from whom it raises funds, the companies it also contacts for donations, the politicians who can relieve suffering by new legislation, the national media who push forward the reform process, local media for publicizing fund-raising events, and the charity's actual beneficiaries. If the charity is exclusively local, audience numbers are fairly small. If it is a worldwide charity like Oxfam, its audience is also international.

As we have mentioned, even we individuals must organize to communicate our needs and desires to 'audiences' who can help. In personal communications, though, there is room to convey a strong sense of ourselves. Parents will accept our tantrums because they love us; friends expect our personality to come across in our day-to-day communications, because that is what makes us endearing to them. A teacher or lecturer might tolerate a certain amount of youthful insolence from us because we are at school to develop and learn, and making mistakes along the way is a part of the experience. In all these cases, we enjoy the luxury of selfishness in our self-expression. The temptation to selfishness remains strong when we enter public relations. We have something to say. Surely, then, people will automatically pay attention to wonderful us, just like our friends, teachers and parents? They won't. Public relations differs from personal relations. First, the audience does not necessarily have to listen. They will have other demands on their time and money. They may never even have heard of us. Why should they be interested in us or our organization? If we really want them to listen, we have to put their collective preferences and personality before our own. We have to find out about the kind of people they are. We have to keep their own needs and desires in mind in order to have a chance of success. That is, in the last analysis, exactly how we have been communicated to by organizations for most of our lives.

Whether you know it or not, you are a public-relations audience every day, almost from the moment you creep from your bed, and stumble into the shower. You turn on the tap, maybe aware that your tapwater has aluminium and fluoride in it, aluminium as a clearant and fluoride for healthy teeth. If you are, it is because you, the water user, have been targeted by freedom groups, health groups and water companies as part of a debate to influence opinion on the safety of these additives – is aluminium responsible for Alzheimer's disease? You shower, with the aid of your Body Shop soap made from only 'natural' ingredients, and afterwards use cosmetics that have not been tested on animals. You made these purchasing decisions because for many years messages were sent through the media by environmentalists and anti-vivisectionists. The Body Shop itself runs student tours of its 'green' production facilities.

Time for breakfast. A bowl of muesli and semi-skimmed milk, because you as a western consumer have been exposed to medical literature and intense media support for healthy eating to cut the risk of heart disease. On the other hand, you may defiantly pour cream in every direction and be equally aware of the health risk. The table off which you are eating is made of pine. The pine came from a forest where one tree is planted for every other one chopped down. This information was printed on a label and attached to the table before it was purchased. It is part of a public-relations initiative by logging companies to prevent harsh Government legislation restricting the quota of trees they can fell. You open the newspaper. The lead story is a public-sector strike. The Union's leader has held a press conference. She puts her case well, with some sharp, snappy observations. You rarely agree with strikes, but you feel you can identify with her personality, which is exactly what her communications adviser hoped would happen when he arranged the conference and rehearsed the spokeswoman. You turn to the financial section to check your family's modest investments. An enthusiastic report about a certain company encourages small investors to buy into it, as the financial public relations consultancy who introduced the journalist to the story hoped it would do. You feed the cat, with a certain brand of health-conscious pet food, recommended by your vet (incidentally, why did he recommend it? The expert endorsements and scientific papers the company sent to him certainly helped). You have a short chat with your sister. She is choosing a university to attend in September. One place in particular catches her attention. It is written about from the point of view of the student. Each course is profiled by one undergraduate, and one former graduate. The application process is explained in a cartoon strip at the end. The layout and photography are instantly appealing, and pre-application tours are available, with overnight accommodation on college property. Students themselves will show her round, and the day will begin and end with a talk by faculty representatives and student-liaison personnel. It is still early in the year, but she feels that this university might suit her. She is so enthusiastic, in fact, that she paints the university in glowing terms – thus making you the attentive recipient of a third-party endorsement, and your sister the (unpaid) endorser.

You leave for work, stopping en route to cast a vote in the local election. It's a tough choice. Both candidates have spent the past month making countless personal appearances, including one at your office. There have been several radio interviews, and a much publicized dinner for one of the candidates attended by local celebrities. What impressed you the most, though, was the visit by one of the candidates to a deprived area of the city. He was dressed casually, and spent his time talking to local people and residents' committees. Afterwards, he made a short speech in front of a community centre and held a news conference announcing his policy proposals. You like his informal approach and his way of explaining ideas. Although you would gladly lower all politicians into a pit of irritated scorpions, you suspect that this candidate is the best of a bad bunch, shrug, and award him your vote. Needless to say, the event that attracted your attention was planned and devised by the candidate's communications team in a last-minute attempt to win over undecided or apathetic voters.

But it is after you have arrived at work that your day as a public-relations audience really begins. For most of it you are an 'internal' audience – the target of motivating messages from the organization that employs you. It is a multinational, a fact which becomes apparent as soon as you enter the lobby. The dominant colour and the company logo are exactly the same in every one of the company's 51 office lobbies worldwide. You sift through a pile of faxes from colleagues in Beijing, Paris and Johannesburg: the heading, the layout of the paper, all similar, designed on the recommendation of internal communications consultants in an effort to forge a single identity and shared commitment among the corporation's 32,000 culturally and linguistically distinct employees, scattered across 40 different countries on four continents. At lunch, you flip through the company's magazine. Copies are deliberately left in recreation areas for employees to pick up in idle moments. It's a monthly, boasting high-quality photographs and well-written articles. The feature you like best is the one that profiles a day in the life of a company employee elsewhere in the world. Not just their work, but their life, their expectations, their customs and beliefs. This is an attempt by internal communications executives to promote a smooth working relationship between employees from completely different backgrounds.

After the break, you attend a meeting to discuss management changes. There have also been redundancies, and the reasons for them, and the implications for those remaining in work, are fully explained by your line manager, with time at the end for questions. It is a surprisingly successful professional presentation from a usually awkward person. The redundancies have left a bad taste in the mouth, and a lingering concern that more are coming, but at the end of the meeting you grudgingly credit the management for candour. Some even agree that maybe the changes were inevitable. Meanwhile, the line manager reports to his director that morale and employee response to his presentation were on the whole positive, and should help end the rumours that have been circulating around the office. A week earlier, he was given presentation training and rehearsed for the meeting, along with other line managers, by public-relations counsellors. The main elements of the presentation – the script, slides, anticipated questions and answers ('Q&As') – were prepared by a consultancy working closely with the corporate-communications team and the board of directors.

Late afternoon. You adjourn to a television studio run by an independent production company, in collaboration with a public-relations consultancy specializing in corporate communications. For a fee, your company rents time from the station to create live video-links with its representatives around the world. The meeting is to discuss the marketing of a new engineering product developed at your company's Oslo facility. The cameras tie in engineers from Norway, and marketing and public-relations executives from several locations including Sydney and Hong Kong. Another camera is trained on the new product as an engineer explains its features. Visibility makes its design and function easier to understand, and enables the basics of a centralized marketing plan and budget to be developed on the spot, with plenty of account being taken of differences in local approaches.

Back home. You switch on the television to catch the early evening news, and resume your identity as an 'external' audience, receiving public-relations messages from organizations to which you do not belong. The top story is the collapse of a new hotel in a popular holiday resort. Thirty people are feared dead. Several hundred more are injured. A speaker for a local residents' association that had apparently opposed the building development now appears in front of the cameras to damn the hotel chain for short-cuts in construction with unqualified cheap labour. The company, she adds for good measure, has made no contribution to local community life since it built its unwelcome hotel in the vicinity. It is a powerful piece. The newsreader says that the hotel chain had been contacted but had refused to comment. Instead, it issued a legal statement pointing out that the company had obeyed the construction code and placing full confidence in the emergency services. The apparent callousness of the reaction makes a negative impression on you, and – as you can see from his expression – on the newscaster. Neither you nor the newscaster know that, working under intense pressure, a public-relations expert in crisis communications had prepared a crisis-communications strategy for the hotel chain that stressed sincerity and openness. It was instantly rejected by the Chief Executive, who preferred lying low to standing in front of a hostile and chaotic press conference; and by the company lawyer, who worried that expressing regret sounded too much like an admission of legal guilt. Public hostility is filling the hole made by the company's silence. It is slow to react, and without any public-relations plan to help it present its messages, and more importantly, retain the trust of employees, customers and investors.

You drink a decaffeinated coffee, read a chapter from a new novel purchased after a personal appearance by the author at a nearby book shop, and retire to bed grateful that you are not in the hotel business. Tomorrow, you must get up and be a public-relations audience all over again.

THEM, THE ORGANIZATION

The personalities of people and of the organizations to which they belong depend on several uncontrollables: inheritance, accidents, and occasionally pre-meditated decisions. The corporate identity of banks, and later of all great institutions of finance, owes much to the taste, religion, and capacity for public relations of the bankers of the Italian Renaissance. They were concerned as any modern bank with sending the right message to their audiences. Today, the banks send messages through their architecture, their publicity literature, through cultivating a close relationship with politicians, through motivating their employees, through sponsorship of the arts.[3] The skylines of many large cities, for instance, are deeply influenced by banking and finance. The City of London has its Square Mile, Paris boasts the high rises of La Défense. Even the core of small cities are stamped dramatically by the symbols of finance. Toronto's downtown includes, among others, the white tower of the bank of Montreal, the three black towers of the Toronto Dominion bank, and the slender pink granite comb named for the Bank of Nova Scotia. In cities everywhere, the image of banking is generously conveyed through buildings designed to attract respect and custom as dramatic symbols of power, potency and permanence. In the smaller towns of the western world, the same banks try to reflect a completely different personality, one that local users might appreciate. A traditional nineteenth-century bank building hints at continuity, prudence and security. A small, modern, well lit and plainer building tries to convey a bank's approachability, informality and desire to reflect the expectations of its regular customers.

Why is our idea of a bank's identity different from our idea of, for example, a school? Both institutions wish us to make different but important investments with them. Both need to show that they are secure places for us to deposit our money or our children, and both deal with exactly the same people, as parents or account holders. Why then, should they project differing personalities? One reason is that we behave differently in our relations with both organizations. The banks and schools know this, and behave differently to us. Parents' associations are considered to be an important sign that a school values the opinions and ideas of the community. Many school public-relations campaigns are about building public trust through participation. If a bank called regular meetings of us, its customers, and asked for ideas and opinions about how it should be running itself, we would probably wonder why it asked us about a job it should be expert at, and take our business very speedily elsewhere. Alternatively, we do not extend to a school the faith that we are ready to place in the hands of a bank. We would be suspicious and concerned for our children's future if a distant approach was taken by their school. If our bank is located in an expensive highrise of glass and steel, or an ornate, traditional stone edifice lavish with marble, we feel confident that it knows how to manage our money. If a school were to do the same, we might not feel as confident, and maybe would question its ability to use our money wisely. Whatever the logical similarities between organizations, they must be ready to communicate with us in very different ways.

Organizations have lives of their own, although they are staffed by human beings and theoretically exist to serve us. The organization is a simple idea, developed to meet human needs, that has grown complex in order to accommodate the new technologies we have developed to regulate our lives and to feed our habits and tastes, which seem to change so constantly. They are a profoundly human idea, and the intricacy of the organizations humans have developed separates them from the simpler structures automatically inherited by other species.

If that rough definition of organizations was entirely accurate, there would be no need for them to use public relations, except for communicating simple information about the services we can expect to receive. But humans want to invest elements of their own complex characters in the organizations they use, and this has meant that organizations grow personalities of their own. Occasionally, an organization will conduct research, and try to assume the personality that users or supporters expect it to have. Other organizations are confident or old enough to have established secure, symbolic, identities of their own that – like Rolls Royce – influence the views and aspirations of many people.

The interconnected identities of audience and organization, and the constant search by one for the other's approval, have had a powerful effect on public relations. Complicated and specialized initiatives are constantly being launched to implant an organization's view of its identity into its public; and the bigger this task, the greater the need for a public-relations function that is free, above and outside the many other functions of the organization. From the soup of inheritance, accident, and careful planning, public relations must extract the messages that will justly reflect an organization's desired identity. The public image of Body Shop differs from that of Royal Dutch Shell.

They aim at different audiences, or at least at different aspects of the same consumer's personality, and so must use different tools to communicate their images. When Anita Roddick of the Body Shop establishes a scheme to assist threatened tribes in Amazonia, or hosts a television programme about global warming, she is telling us something very definite about her company's objectives.

Would the Chief Executive Officer of Shell be spending his valuable time usefully if he promoted his company in the same way? Shell is a much older company. Few of us know the Chief Executive's name or are likely to be interested in knowing it. A public announcement that Shell is sponsoring a Body Shop-style investigation into global warming or – in the case of Brent Spar -the best way to dispose of an old oil rig is liable to arouse consumer, politicians' and environmentalist suspicions of bias, of an oil corporation prepared to twist the findings to serve itself. Yet Shell's scientists could well be doing more than Body Shop technologists to solve the problem of global warming. Shell is not the same sort of company as the Body Shop. It is older, well-established, massive, rich. It has a tradition of projecting itself strictly through its own name and product, not through the personality and beliefs of whoever happens to be in charge. Shell supplies a vital resource to us customers who may, by the way, enjoy Body Shop products as well. We simply have different priorities when we go shopping for the goods the two organizations sell. Perhaps we have bought Body Shop cosmetics made from natural rainforest products; maybe we feel satisfied to be helping the environment in this way, as we drive our cars into Shell forecourts to fill them up and join the late afternoon queue of traffic leaving town.

As far apart as they are in the way they communicate and the messages they send, both companies have two things in common: they are successful, and they depend on communications to serve up ideas about what they represent. Their opponents or competitors, meanwhile, are doing exactly the same, a fact that allows us to choose between the organizations we need. Because competitors must seek out and identify new publics to communicate with, they become increasingly dependent on audience expectations and opinions. The steady growth of newer audiences to engage is a feature of our democratic, participative century. It has meant that would-be communicators were forced to change their methods. Fledgling campaign groups were the first to do so, and they gave reluctant and slow organizations an important lesson about adapting to incorporate public relations. In Britain, the conservative National Farmers Union (NFU) is arguably the single most effective non-government organization in British, possibly European Union, politics. Its communications structure is an excellent subject of study as it has, to date, been highly successful, much copied but never bettered by corporate and other non-government organizations. Its members were originally small farmers, not the lords and gentry who had traditionally been agriculture's political representatives . That class of people started to decline in numbers in the First World War thanks to heavy taxation. The NFU's members, in contrast, were offered emergency financial incentives to grow food. This enriched them, and forced them into a closer relationship with the state. The Union had to organize to address the new needs that this created. It rapidly expanded until the war's end in 1918, by which time it included a large portion of the farming population. NFU leaders were painfully aware of their lack of contacts, and their near-total inexperience as communicators in the world of public affairs. What to do? Wisely, they took a series of steps that have more or less been followed by almost every lobby group since.

They began by appointing someone they called a 'lobbyist'. This was something fairly new, but coping with the pressing new responsibilities of novices like the NFU undoubtedly required the services of a paid professional adviser, with a background in government, who knew how to communicate an inexperienced organization's messages to political audiences. The NFU also pioneered the idea of a wholly separate communications function within an organization. It established a parliamentary, press and publicity committee, which quickly became one of the leading forces in the Union. A county branch system was built, designed to ensure that the NFU kept in touch with the opinion of its members. Lastly, the committee took over a small newspaper, the *Mark Lane Express*. Their early, inexperienced, messages tended to be blunt and unpopular in the urban world, but by the middle of the 1930s the Union had turned its public-relations machine into a powerful political force, in constant touch with its internal membership, and extremely influential in Government. It was so tightly organized that for many years politicians from rural districts worried that they might lose elections if they went against the Union: quite an achievement for an organization that at its largest was around ninety thousand strong in a land of fifty-odd million.

While the NFU was making public relations a central part of its activities, the mass circulating newspapers were busily prising more conservative-minded companies away from their traditional view that their business was nobody else's. 'Public be damned', the American multi-millionaire Vanderbilt is supposed to have said in an injudicious moment. With an attitude of that sort firmly cemented into business conduct, it was hardly surprising that the first corporate public-relations efforts were regarded with suspicion. Nevertheless, Ivy Lee showed what could be done when he closed the vast gap separating an apparently ruthless mining company from the bad opinion of the American newspapers. Lee restructured the public face of a defensive, silent, and criticized firm in the course of a vicious labour dispute, and persuasively re-presented its messages to the press. The early clients for public relations tended to be locked into similar confrontations. They included private utilities, fearful of municipal take-over. Their methods, such as those developed by US railroad companies fighting Federal interference at the end of the nineteenth century, are now standard to communications. It is known that the inter-war campaign of the electricity and other utility companies included: 'press releases, pamphlets, public talks, school programs, employment of college professors, student internships and memberships in civic clubs and community organizations'.[4] In 1932, presidential candidate Franklin D. Roosevelt – himself a master at communications – was one of those who, when faced with advocacy for an issue they do not agree with, target the medium rather than the message itself. He accused the companies of 'lies and falsehood', of placing propaganda in the national newspapers 'bought and paid for by certain great private utility corporations'.[5] Nevertheless, shaping raw information by paid publicity specialists, instead of exclusively by newspapers, has become a characteristic of our times. Lee and other pioneers conclusively changed the structure of an organization's relations with its audience. Lee himself is considered to be one of the 'fathers' of public relations; his working descendants can now even be found in the sorts of organizations that would have noisily opposed the ones he represented.

NOTES

1 Poe, Edgar Allan. 'Man of the Crowd'. *Selected Writings* (London: Penguin, 1980) p 188.
2 Orwell, George. *Homage to Catalonia* (London: Penguin, reprinted 1980. First published 1938) p 236.
3 It is unsurprising that Catholic, civic Italy is now constructing football stadia. Some of them are magnificent enough to match the high design standards set by Italians in organized religion and finance, and send similar messages. 'An architectural wonder which is seems not sacrilegious at all to compare with *Il Duomo* – Milan's cathedral – the San Siro is part of the tradition by which power is expressed through buildings,' wrote a journalist visiting the home of AC Milan football club. San Siro belongs to Silvio Berlusconi, the communications millionaire and Italian Prime Minister in the mid-1990s. O'Hagan, Simon. 'In search of the heart of Europe'. *Independent on Sunday*, 2 October 1994, Sport, p 7.
4 Jordan, Myron K. 'FDR's condemnation of electric utility public relations'. *Public Relations Review*, XV, No 2 (Summer 1989) p 42.
5 Rosenman, Samuel I. (ed.). *The Public Papers and Addresses of Franklin D. Roosevelt*, vol. I. (New York: Random House, 1938) p 729, cited in Jordan, 'FDR's condemnation'.

CHAPTER FIVE

Original People,
Original Words, Original Ideas

If, as I suppose, sympathy with all sorts and conditions
of men, and tolerance of human diversity be an attribute
of civilised life, then Rembrandt was one of the great
prophets of civilisation.[1] –
Lord Clark

It may already be clear to you that contemporary public relations shares many of the characteristics Lord Clark ascribes to Rembrandt. It too must demonstrate 'tolerance of human diversity' and embrace 'all sorts and conditions of men'. The difference is that, fortunately for us, Rembrandt placed them in the service of his own selfish genius. Public relations places them in the service of organizations. Rembrandt concentrated those characteristics in himself to create art that still carries meaning. In public relations the same elements are distributed in more modest quantities among thousands of practitioners, some terrible, others brilliant, but who, taken as a whole, shape with far greater if less pre-meditated profundity than Rembrandt the way we, citizens of the consumer age, see our own civilization.

We often measure our civilization through the way it is communicated to us. One day, you may be retained to manage the public relations of a well-known company that plans to fire three thousand employees in order to cut costs. These people have performed well. They have mortgages, families, self-respect. They have legal entitlements: a pension scheme and a payoff package. A straightforward announcement of the sacking would not settle these things. In any case, if it was only a matter of making a certain number of people redundant, the task could be left to the human-resources department. In reality, many other audiences important to the company are also involved, each with different requirements. Shareholders and investors will need to be convinced that the company remains in good shape. The media might want to cover the redundancies, how will they be handled? Politicians may query the increased unemployment in their districts. What if the redundancies are occurring in different countries? Last but not least, what about the survivors, those employees who are not fired? How will you communicate with them about the incident, and what can you do to ensure that employee morale, which is closely linked to output, does not suffer?

Communications contracts like this can involve six- or seven-figure sums because clients have high expectations. They expect that the attitudes or actions of the audiences that matter to them will be affected in the desired way: perhaps by an appropriate schedule of mass redundancies that enables the organization to restructure for the future. Whatever it is, reaching the ideal outcome requires perceptive communicators who, to succeed, must in their strategic decisions respect and endorse society's codes of conduct. It is a paradox that this respect is not always gained by conforming to set procedures. Many times it is wiser to ignore standard practice. Often, it is better to cut imaginatively through the distractions and contradictions surrounding the subject that is holding our attention, pull out the single message that matters to an organization and present it in a refreshing way to an information-glutted audience. A tank invaded the City of London in December 1993. It was quickly brought to a halt by heavily armed police and expectant media. In it they found, not a terrorist, but a man who wanted to publicize his indignation at a local council's refusal to let him mount a fish trophy above his house. Admittedly, a fish trophy is not a matter of high import, except to the tank-driving resident and maybe his long-suffering council. Nevertheless, he had the wit to draw attention to this mundane topic in an interesting fashion: not by writing an outraged letter to the council (how many of those do they get a week?), but by climbing into a tank and taking it to London.[2] That degree of imagination produces, without doubt, the best sort of public relations. It is true that such tactics would not suit regular communications problems. The options for improving the public relations of a merchant bank, for example, might seem less promising. But it is not necessarily true that a commercial relationship, however unpromising the problem, need diminish our creative power. Like other great artists, Rembrandt painted for a fee. Many of his finest pictures were commercial ventures executed for well-informed and cultivated clients. They continue to communicate meaning to us after five centuries. We are moved both by the *Anatomy class of Dr Tulp*, and by the *Night Watch*. We regard them as pinnacles of human accomplishment.

Rembrandt laboured, and dared, and became a great artist. He could not have done so merely by copying others, or by slavishly following the recommendations of a textbook, perhaps entitled 'Six Steps To Producing Art That Will Live Forever'. In the same way, nobody will be an excellent and fulfilled public-relations practitioner by relying exclusively on guides that promise to equip them with the right technical tools. Public relations has had such guides available for a long time. Many are thoroughly excellent, others deeply flawed. They take the complex and changing impulses that drive individuals and organizations to talk with each other, and deal with them by showing how the tools of the trade apply to this organic, shifting mass. This desire to make technical sense of public relations – the 'how to' – has made

vital contributions to its discipline and procedures, and is now readily accessible to public-relations students via manuals, journals, certain university
courses and the accumulation of experience. These are the instructors and
drill sergeants of the practice, but they are not enough. We are not robots.
'How to' is a way of showing how to open the door to public-relations, but
as David Dozier has persuasively warned:

> Practitioners frequently demand that university curricula teach public
> relations majors to 'write, write, write!' In terms of preparing public
> relations undergraduates for their first six months in public relations
> work, the prudent university would immerse public relations
> undergraduates in nothing but writing. Indeed, writing is an important
> technical skill. However, such prudence would condemn public
> relations to death as a profession . . . The same practitioners who view
> public relations as a cluster of technical communication skills are
> among those who lament other crises in public relations. Those crises
> involve encroachment and practitioner exclusion from decision
> making.[3]

Intelligent explorations of original thinking in communications are harder
to find; yet who would not agree that original thinking broadens the role of
public relations, breeds personal satisfaction and magnifies a successful
accomplishment? There must be a place for imagination because, as I have
said, the best public-relations work can – like the finest art – have a deep
influence on people. This inspirational black hole is one of the reasons why
senior management positions in public relations are sometimes occupied by
professionals from other areas.[4] There is of course no doubt that experience
of other disciplines can help to solve specific communications problems, and
even widen the possibilities open to public relations in general. Interestingly,
many successful generals have possessed a keen instinct for imaginative
communications. The military historian John Keegan has concluded that 'a
gift for public relations is a necessary, even if not sufficient, element of gen-
eralship'.[5] Antagonists and supporters of Field Marshal Montgomery of
Alamein are equally ready to concede that he had a 'perfect grasp of public
relations'.[6] Montgomery knew his audience. In the Second World War he
commanded huge conscript armies of civilians drawn from every walk of
life. The army was not their chosen home and they were less liable than professionals to follow orders without question. Montgomery set himself the
task of communicating the goals and targets of his strategy to his soldiers in
lengthy, exhausting but to his mind indispensable meetings. 'Monty said
wars were won by soldiers' morale,' a journalist recalled. 'Morale came with
confidence in the generals. Confidence only came with knowledge.
Knowledge needed familiarity.'[7] To the public he conveyed the impression

that he commanded a well-organized army that cared about the welfare and lives of the troops. Thanks to his keen sense of public relations as well as his military abilities, he became one of the best known personalities of the war. 'Confidence in the high command', he wrote later, was essential. 'I wanted to see the soldiers and, probably more important, I wanted them to see me; I wanted to speak to them and try to gain their trust and confidence'.[8] A telling sign of the value Montgomery placed on communications was his commitment, in the midst of D-Day preparations, to an intensive schedule of travel for days on end across the country to address two and often three parades a day, up to 30,000 soldiers in total. Montgomery paid careful attention to ensuring that the men gather round informally to get a good look at him. He knew exactly what he was doing. 'This inspection of the men by me, and of me by them, took some little time; but it was good value for all of us. It was essential that I gained their confidence. I had to begin with their curiosity'.[9] Radio, too, formed part of his public-relations strategy: 'I'm the first general in history who can speak quietly and be heard by every single man'.[10]

Another famous wartime leader, Bill Slim, commanded the Imperial Army in Burma. He too, perhaps because of his early career as a Birmingham school teacher, stressed the value of 'informal talks and contacts between troops and commanders',[11] and spent roughly a third of his precious time in such activities. He carefully organized his other public relations, and schooled his senior officers to do likewise. His classic strategy stressed the need to send a common and coherent message, not an easy task in a massive multinational organization containing diverse peoples from Asia, Africa and Europe, and with many leaders spread over a large and lonely area of operations. Nevertheless, he had strong views about communications, wanted his generals to 'increase these activities' and wished to 'unite them in a common approach to the problem, in the points they would stress, and in the action they would take to see that principles became action, not merely words'.[12]

In the pursuit of the unexpected and inspired, it must never be forgotten that at root it remains important to know how to 'write, write, write!' Slim realized the value of good writing. He placed great weight, for example, on producing a successful 'in-house' newspaper for his soldiers. Good public-relations practitioners must be able to find the written words that match their audiences and messages. Again, reverting to our comparison with Rembrandt, 'creativity' and 'originality' in public relations writing need not be defined by admiring the concentrated genius of one particular writer. It may be defined instead as the ability of a particular piece of writing to strike its intended targets. To help us consider this matter, two descriptions of the same subject are offered:

1. What a city Lyons is! Talk about people feeling, at certain unlucky times, as if they had tumbled from the clouds! Here is a whole town

that is tumbled, anyhow, out of the sky; having been first caught up, like other stones that tumble down from that region, out of fens and barren places, dismal to behold! The two great streets through which the two great rivers dash, and all the little streets whose name is Legion, were scorching, blistering, and sweltering. The houses, high and vast, dirty to excess, rotten as old cheeses, and as thickly peopled.[13]

2. Today, from its tastefully restored vieille ville to its modern commercial centers, Lyons offers excellent museums, marathon nightlife, a friendly student population, world-renowned cuisine and affordable accommodations. This attractive, cultivated city merits an extended visit.[14]

In literary terms the first passage, written by Charles Dickens in 1846, possesses a higher degree of personal creativity. It is a fascinating and unusual jumble of images. Nevertheless, from a public-relations perspective, both accounts are extremely successful. They are written for different audiences, and each has hit its particular target. Dickens, a noted and best-selling author then and now, was writing for himself, but that is precisely what his audience wanted. They wanted his thoughts and ideas about a place most of them were not going to visit. Television and photography did not exist to supplement their vision of Lyons. Dickens was, most probably, the only source they had, so they depended on his imagination and powers of recall. The second account, written for *Let's Go France* in 1994, is humdrum by comparison. A collation of facts, 'travelese' and functional language. Unimaginative but, to any public-relations practitioner, also on target. The readers of *Let's Go*, a top-selling travel guide, have an entirely different set of needs from those of the original readers of Dickens. They are reading about Lyons because they might decide to go there. Beyond a smattering of atmospherics, they are not seeking a deeply coloured picture of the city, which they could in any case see for themselves. Their need is for information that helps them to make a choice, then make the most of their own visit. They are not necessarily interested in whether the writer thinks Lyons looks like a rotting cheese. They are interested in knowing quickly whether it is worth visiting, and where to stay and what to see. The needs and expectations of the two audiences differ, so the writing must differ.

Knowledge of the ways in which the same subject can be adapted to audiences is essential to public-relations. If you, as a public-relations practitioner, were responsible for a campaign to attract corporations to Lyons, how would you present the city? Phrases like 'dirty to excess' will not attract business executives, nor will a handbook showing them how to travel from Lyons's main station to the cheapest hotel. They speak a different language, they require a different content. Commercial audiences want to hear about other aspects of the city: the qualifications of its workforce, its rates of tax and potential investment costs. The public-relations programme will need to show them why Lyons beats Boulogne, or Frankfurt, or Barcelona. Books will not be the right way to get your written message to them. Brochures, speeches, tours, and video scripts may be more useful. Perhaps news releases are necessary, aimed at appropriate media such as business journals, and the financial sections of daily newspapers. A media-relations campaign may also be necessary to build more personal links with relevant correspondents.

News releases to journalists are the most commonly known public-relations tool. Many journalists like to be cynical about releases in particular, and about public relations's treatment of facts in general, but the truth is that the two either enjoy or endure a close relationship.[15] Public relations widens a journalist's pool of usable stories. Some practitioners, like the press officer at 10 Downing Street, regulate journalists' access to a permanently important news source. For public-relations practitioners, newspapers are still the preferred route when sending a message to large numbers of people. For all these reasons the release is an old favourite. One reason it is less popular with the journalists themselves is that its quality can vary drastically. Journalists can, unsurprisingly, read and write. It is their trade, and they do not appreciate badly written releases. Furthermore, all journalists, from a junior local newspaper reporter to a network television news reader, expect to spend a large part of their day staring at a small mountain of press releases. Assuming they have the time to read them all, what will then make them reach into the pile, pull out the release that we wrote, and actually use it? We plan to make them pick our release because:

- We wrote it especially to reflect their interests.

- It is written to resemble, not a hard-selling advertisement, but a finished newspaper article with short, punchy paragraphs and sentences. It is not an advertisement.

We have written for our newspaper-reading audience as appropriately as Dickens wrote for his loyal readers. In fact, we are more adaptable than Dickens, because we can alter our writing to serve the requirements of several audiences.

Public relations is not mathematics. It will never unearth a series of standard steps to fix all communications problems. It is fortunately less predictable than that, because it is able to work with the contradictory and unique personalities, desires and behaviour of us, the public. That is why public relations seeks out images and sounds as well as writing. That is why we must return to Rembrandt, and the painting *Bathsheba with King David's letter*, completed in 1654. The woman was Hendrickje Stoffels, Rembrandt's common law wife who died six years after posing for the picture. Three and a half centuries later, we know that the dark, dimpled area Rembrandt noticed on Hendrickje's left breast is a sign of advanced breast cancer.

In November 1990, the painting became the centre of a four-month information campaign encouraging women to have mammograms, launched in Sydney by the Medical Benefits Fund of Australia. Rembrandt, perpetually in debt, detected no need for public relations. Perhaps it says something for the vision of public relations that it found an original need for Rembrandt.

A neurosurgeon once described the challenge of his profession to me in terms that should strike a chord with any public-relations practitioner. For 'neurosurgeon', read 'public-relations practitioner'. For 'glucose', read 'messages'. 'We can', he said, 'track the uptake of glucose in the brain. When we ask a patient to think of beautiful things – a castle, woods, a lake – we can pursue the glucose to the part of the brain that is being activated. When we ask them to think of something completely different – hate, murder, war – the glucose is carried to another part of the brain. Patients can imagine. They can produce images and ideas without having to see or hear them. They don't reproduce exact photocopies of other people's experiences. That is not what we are: our spirit, soul, personality. Neurosurgeons now know something about how people work. We don't know why. We just can't make the link between "person" and brain – that's why we turn to philosophy. You cannot understand neurosurgery if all you do is treat it as a technical skill. Other surgery is about restoring patients to what they were before – before they fell ill. A heart transplant restores the heart. A liver transplant restores the liver. The patient can function again – that is a technical job. The brain is different. How, exactly, do we re-connect the brain to understand images and ideas? There is no instruction manual for that.'

NOTES

1 Clark, Kenneth. *Civilisation* (London: Penguin, 1987) p 143.
2 *The Economist*, 11 December 1993, p 67.
3 Dozier, David M. 'Planning and evaluation in PR Practice'. *Public Relations Review*, pp 20-21.
4 Lesley Philip, cited in Dozier, 'Planning and Evaluation'.
5 Keegan, John. 'Louis takes the blame'. *Daily Telegraph*, 23 July 1994, p 17.
6 Barnett, Correlli. *The Desert Generals* (Bloomington, USA: Indiana University Press, 1982 edition) p 260.
7 'The Allies have landed'. *Radio Times*, 4-10 June 1994, p 36.
8 Montgomery of Alamein. *The Memoirs of Field-Marshal Montgomery* (London: Collins, 1958) p 223.
9 Ibid.
10 *Radio Times*, op. cit.
11 Slim, William. *Defeat into Victory* (London: Cassell, 1957) p 187.
12 Ibid., p 188.
13 Dickens, Charles. *American Notes and Pictures from Italy* (Oxford: 1966, first published 1846) p 270.
14 *Let's Go France* (New York: St Martin's Press, 1994) p 526.
15 In 1991, Jericho Promotions Inc., a New York public-relations firm, conducted a mail survey of 2432 Canadian and US journalists. 'Given a list of animals, and asked to choose which is "most like a PR person?" 71 per cent said weasel, 11 per cent fox, 2 per cent dog and 1 per cent worm.' At the same time, '81 per cent said they needed PR people; 38 per cent said they get half their stories from them; 31 per cent said they relied on them for information on five to ten stories a week; 15 per cent said they relied on them for more than ten stories; and 17 per cent said they used PR people on every story.'

CHAPTER SIX

Issues Management

Selling ideas is different from selling soap.[1] Margaret Thatcher

In February 1994, residents of Wanstead in England, erected barricades in five houses to protest against a planned motorway extension. New-agers and veteran environmental activists arrived to support the middle-class inhabitants of this respectable London suburb. Banners were hung out of the windows, proclaiming the 'independent state of Wanstonia'. When 600 police officers arrived, the besieged protesters pulled out a contact list of journalists and manned the telephones. The ensuing coverage communicated the anti-road message to a national audience, which was, of course, the whole purpose of the protest.[2] Without the accompanying public relations, the event would have been a waste of time. Nobody would have heard about it, or been influenced by it. But once the press list had been prepared, the journalists called and the photographs taken, the event was part of an intensifying public battle against road construction in the UK. The protesters, of course, use different forms of public relations from those of their road-constructing opponents. The anti-road movement relies heavily on sending messages through direct action, from activists fighting the march of tarmac in organizations like M11 Action Group, Save our Solsbury, or any of the other 250 groups networking through an advisory organization called Alarm UK. It is clearly 'an organised and structured crusade', as a recent report observed; effective too, since 'their ability to stage a publicity campaign is obvious'.[3] The A27 Action Group, for instance, has eight committees including a press group and a lobby group.[4] Road builders and civil servants send their messages more discreetly, in press conferences, private media interviews, meetings with residents and local authorities, and meetings with Government ministers. The idea of executives and administrators barricading themselves in their offices in support of roads, or leading public protests against the police, is plainly ludicrous. It would be dismissed as self-interest, or criticized as illegal and irresponsible. Clearly, the public relations that works for one organization will not always work for another, even if the issue is the same.

Different as these two approaches to public relations are, they both grapple with a social – instead of a strictly commercial – problem. This area of public relations practice has its preferred communications activities; unsurprisingly it goes by many names, including 'public affairs' and 'government relations', but perhaps the most generic is 'issues management'. The issue at Wanstead was a new road scheme. Elsewhere, it might be a proposal for tough labelling legislation, or a company's race-relations record. It could be as local as Wanstead, or as global as cancer or the ozone layer. Issues management deals with matters of public concern that might, if allowed to develop, retard the effectiveness of an organization. It is a flourishing segment of public-relations practice. It obliges its practitioners to get to grips with fascinating and complex problems before even beginning to communicate messages about them; it builds programmes designed to work for several years, or to drive an urgent message home in a few urgent weeks.

It is popularly believed that public relations and press releases always go together. The public and occasionally practitioners take the view of the poet Brendan Behan who is meant to have commented: 'all publicity is good publicity – except your obituary'. But it is not always the objective of public relations to secure blanket coverage. In fact, one justification for public relations is that it is highly discriminating, seeking out the best and most economical means of reaching its publics. On occasion, this may certainly require mass publicity, but not all public-relations tasks are about urging people to put Holes in their pockets, or involve the intense and exhausting publicity expected by the managers of an election campaign. This is true of issues management. Although it is closely connected in popular opinion to marketing hype and drumming up media enthusiasm, the growth in public relations owes a good deal to its skill in restraining heavy and critical media coverage. For the main part, issues management is less about selling cans of beans, and more about re-sealing cans of worms. Media coverage is often seen as a sign that an organization's issues management is going in the wrong direction. It is just one among many communications tools capable of reaching a remarkably varied range of audiences numbered in dozens or in hundreds of thousands.

It is easy for unsuspecting companies to flounder in a tide of hostile opinion. For this reason, many people turn to issues communication. A Swiss chemical company recently made plans to store its chemical waste above ground in another country. Local people in that country were opposed to the idea. They naturally worried about the hazards, the effect on land values and on business. On top of the need to change the minds of these publics, the company needed to win permission from the authorities to set up the site. Traditional publicity was obviously not the solution. Newspaper headlines would not encourage contact and the dialogue needed in a small community, nor would it persuade the councillors and residents leading the objections. Instead, the company trained representatives who held meetings with people in the affected district, produced a film that was shown to the local population, and prepared a brochure about the project. When, as in this case, the task of building trust is paramount, small-scale contact is more effective than a shower of press releases sent from afar. By-passing or relegating the role of the media can have other advantages. It permits tighter control of the message by saving it from distortion and extraneous interpretation at the hands of a neutral, hostile or distracted journalist.

Issues management must be ready to address the concerns of its audiences. Issues communicators must advocate, not sell; they must often act with discretion and always with extreme sensitivity; they must be imaginative. They must be sincere, for as the philosopher Nietsche observed: 'Men believe in the truth of all that is seen to be strongly believed in.' Public relations on issues must show conviction to convince others. It must be prepared to open contact with its audiences as early as possible. It must avoid the temptation to indulge in a one-way bombardment of messages, and must be ready to advise dialogue and possibly changes in an organization's practices. It is a subtle, interesting and many-layered form of public relations. More than any other branch of the practice, issues management must address the concerns of its audiences if it is to succeed. It can appear extremely complex and contradictory, partly because the likely impact of an issue on an organization is often hard to assess. It may be of benefit to an organization to 'adopt' an issue and publicly take it over; or, if the issue is felt to represent a risk, a direct physical threat, a very public communications strategy may be necessary to counter it. Imaginative organizations might even combine the two, such as in the gruesome and rare case of the international media coverage given to 'Death' cigarettes – the fashionable brand with a skull on the pack – openly marketed by a small British manufacturer as a cause of lung cancer, and leaving the final choice on the matter to the consumer. A percentage of the profits from Death goes to medical research.

Organizations are interested in issues management because we use our knowledge of issues to reach decisions, and on occasion to take hostile positions. We are exposed to dozens of issues every time we open our newspapers, or listen to broadcast news, quite apart from other sources of information. We respond to this exposure in several ways. At our lowest level of active response to an issue, our opinions – including whether or not we have any – are checked by interested organizations on a regular basis, for example via opinion surveys. Others may be so concerned about an issue that they make a personal, visible stand: refusing to buy products wrapped in too much packaging, not eating foods that contain hydrogenated oils because they believe it contributes to heart disease, signing a petition against dog licensing. At the top level, we might decide to devote a lot of our time to one particular issue, perhaps by attending a public demonstration, or by becoming so involved in the leadership of a particular group that we become a 'key influencer' – a person whose opinions on an issue are valued by the media, and other concerned organizations.[5] All our views and actions, weak or strong, are treated with respect. They are often used by organizations to justify their positions on particular issues. They help to shape messages, to reinforce or undermine corporate confidence, to feed the strength of pressure groups or politicians. Because they need our support, organizations are prepared to spend a lot of public-relations time on influencing our opinions – at times to ensure their continued existence.

It has been mentioned that some issues are not threats, and that some organizations are keen to publicly alert their audiences to them. How does issues management work in these circumstances? In answer, it is helpful to explore the connection between prostate cancer and ice hockey. After many years of investment and research, a large North American drug company produced a drug for patients suffering from prostate cancer. The drug successfully delayed the need for the only available treatment, which was unfortunately castration. The company saw their new development as good news; relief for patients and an alternative form of treatment for doctors. It remained to sell the product to the customer. In this case the customer had two heads: the doctors who stocked and prescribed the drug, and the patients who asked for it. Advertising in medical journals was one obvious tactic. Another was salespeople visiting doctors' surgeries. These are necessary, and occasionally expensive, steps to take. Another option, more imaginative, less expensive and possibly more effective, was to use issues management to stimulate a continuous demand for the new drug. In this regard there was much to learn from the treatment of breast cancer and heart disease. Breast cancer and heart disease have attracted a lot of public attention. Nearly every adult in the western world understands the need to cut cholesterol, but how aware are men of prostate cancer? Prostate cancer is a health issue. It killed 35,000 American males in 1993, comparable to the 46,000 women killed by breast cancer. It received $51 million from the US National Institutes of Health grants in 1994, compared with $299 million for breast cancer research. Public awareness of prostate cancer is low, 'we're twenty years behind the women', said the co-founder of a prostate support group.[6] The condition can be treated if detected quickly, but has received little public attention – partly because of the embarrassing physical examination needed to check for it. Would it not be sensible and responsible to help raise awareness of prostate cancer as a 'silent killer' of mature males? Improved awareness would increase check-ups, the number of early and treatable detections, and ultimately use of the new drug.

The vehicle selected by the company was 'prostate cancer awareness week' designed in co-operation with a public-relations consultancy. With the help of two medical specialists, and a retired North American Ice Hockey star who had himself survived prostate cancer, the company established a group whose sole aim was to communicate two useful messages: that prostate cancer is an important issue; and that it can be detected by regular medical check-ups. The new drug was never mentioned. The audiences: males over the age of forty; and urologists, the specialists responsible for treatment of the prostate. The methods: interviews on local television and radio across North America; articles placed in journals most likely to be read by middle-aged males; brochures and posters were prepared for waiting rooms in hospitals and clinics. The sports star – a hero to many of the middle-aged men targeted by the campaign – committed himself to a series of interviews. He also signed autographs seated in front of a special prostate cancer awareness display at the annual urologists' conference. In this case, public relations worked through a serious issue to the mutual advantage of issue and client.

More often than not, though, an organization resorts to issues management if it feels threatened. A communications programme springing from such a threat might risk the same very public approach taken to support the treatment of prostate cancer. An organization may also do the opposite, find there is nothing to be gained from direct involvement with the issue and, from a distance, back an agreeable third-party better able to convey the messages that appeal to it. Two real but disguised public-relations projects demonstrate these contrasting points, one on behalf of a country, the other on behalf of a corporation. The country in question was confronted by a problem not of its own making, global enough for us to return to later in a slightly different form. Several European Union nations were damaging the country's fish stocks by trawling just outside the country's territorial waters. The damage was twofold: the fish supply was drying up, and the country's fishing fleet felt the pain of reduced catches and revenue. The usual diplomatic manoeuvres were held, but something more was needed to resolve the problem. In order to encourage European Union politicians to make this problem a priority and to take action, the unobstructed lobbying of its fishermen had to be countered by a lobby from other, and preferably well-connected, European citizens. But how many Europeans would actively represent the economic grievances of a rich, and non-European, country? Very few, unless that foreign country prepared an issues-management campaign with a broad message, a message that crossed national lines and won universal support. In this case, the broad message was obviously environmental. There was a natural link between over-fishing and the exhaustion of natural resources; there was a clear link between over-fishing and identification of the 'guilty parties' – the European Union's fishing fleets; there was also an apparently obvious solution -stricter adherence to existing catch quotas. The message was changed to fit the audience.

It is instructive to compare the audiences for fisheries and prostate cancer awareness. The difference explains the diverse approaches required of issues managers. The prostate cancer campaign chased as much publicity as it could, and for good reasons. 'Informed hype' was the best way to reach the massive target audience of every North American male over forty. For over-fishing, the audience is a good deal more select: the small but powerful and well-connected environmental pressure groups at work in Brussels, the European Union's headquarters. A press campaign on the issue would not only risk sacrificing the message to a journalist's story line, it could provoke criticism as an unwarranted intervention in the affairs of other countries by a greedy foreign power. It would also flop because people are frankly not very interested in fish; and because the few who are interested need exposure to specialized information and a lot of direct persuasion in order for them to act. These factors suggested a personal, private, face-to-face strategy. Meetings and presentations were arranged with leading environmentalists. Data and arguments about the environmental implications of over-fishing were presented. Europe's green lobbyists proceeded to activate their own communications network, which confronted Europe's fishing industry with home-grown objections to irresponsible fishing.

Thoughtfully directed and cost-effective issues management helped the aggrieved government to redefine its message from a matter of self-interest into an issue of universal concern, and to put it into the hands of a sympathetic and active audience. In this way, the country was able to by-pass diplomatic negotiations and open a wider debate jointly benefiting its own economic future and to the environment.

While some organizations attempt to raise the profile of certain issues, others feel equally threatened, but have less freedom to manoeuvre. They may have avoided an issue for too long, and allowed their opponents to dominate the debate; they may as a result have fewer opportunities to mould the issue into a more helpful shape. They may also buckle under relentlessly hostile evidence. Organizations in this position cannot expect to turn the tables very easily, and are usually forced to spend a huge amount of effort on damage control. This has been the experience of the tobacco industry. Today, smoking has a bad reputation. The story of the drift in attitude away from smoking as fashionable and towards smoking as a dirty deed is a public-relations tale in itself, spanning the 1950s, 60s and 70s. By the 1980s the tobacco companies in their lead markets of North America and parts of northern Europe were adjusting to tighter restrictions on advertising and high taxation. The public debate had been conducted brilliantly, aggressively and exclusively by the industry's opponents. In the eyes of anti-smoking groups, medical associations, politicians and the media, the traditional tobacco giants were automatically regarded as greedy and ruthless purveyors of death. Finally, after several decades of hoping that the problem would vanish of its own accord, tobacco realized that it faced a massive issues-management problem.

When, following this perilously long delay, the industry decided to band together and face its advancing enemies – as it has a perfect right to do – the terrain was already littered with traps and obstacles. The companies were mistrusted. They were rich and therefore their arguments seemed self-interested. They had not cultivated the media, unlike their opponents. They were, furthermore, multinationals, forced to communicate the same message in a large number of countries – it was essential for them not to contradict themselves anywhere while also taking local prejudices and preferences into account. An issues-management programme of great intricacy was needed.

Medical evidence conclusively linked smoking to cancer and heart disease. About that there could be no further argument. The findings were now so widely accepted that to strongly oppose them would only weaken the tobacco lobby's credibility. The primary smoking issue had been a success for anti-smoking activists, and during the 1980s they sought to build on it. They maintained contacts with the highest levels of Government. They were and are heavily supported by vociferous medical professionals. The light of medical understanding threw out a shadow of social isolation. Many non-smokers found close proximity to a smoker distasteful – not just the smell, but also the deadly fumes drifting from someone else's cigarette. Was inhalation at a distance any different from actually smoking? A body of research appeared to show that 'passive' or 'secondary' smoking indeed affected the health of the bystander. Surely the innocent must be protected? A series of legal actions were brought against tobacco firms by self-proclaimed victims of secondary smoke in North America, Europe and Australia. These events motivated several countries to introduce smoking bans on official premises, and prompted an increase in smoking restrictions imposed by private concerns: airlines, restaurants and offices.

Tobacco might easily have made the elementary mistake of lashing out and attempting to sound off through the media to anyone 'out there'. After all, it had a good deal of general hostility to overcome – and with a lot of pent-up resentment to get off its own chest. It would have been a mistake, because even an issue as enormous as smoking and health revolved around the views of a few knowledgeable publics. They included the publics most likely to be affected by the smoke bans in airlines, offices and restaurants. Statistics indicated that a large number of airline and restaurant customers, and a large number of office employees, were smokers. Tobacco focused its attention on those people. It conducted a two-pronged public-relations campaign that reinforced these facts for the benefit of airline companies, restauranteurs and office managers; and that mobilized smokers themselves with some supportive messages. Tobacco has also attempted to take the controversial act of smoking a cigarette and link it to more attractive principles. These included individual rights (freedom to smoke if anyone chooses); oppression (anti-smokers are trampling on those personal freedoms). They were underpinned by others, more specific: the negative message of flawed evidence (much of the scientific evidence on passive smoking is based on non-medical, statistical data that is contradictory and unproven); and the positive message of courteous smoking (smoke with consideration for the feelings of those around you). In this respect, the tobacco industry's 'broadening' strategy resembled the anonymous government's approach to over-fishing.

Smokers' rights associations were formed or supported in several countries, and local personalities were encouraged to join.[7] Alternative statistical analyses of passive smoking – labelled Environmental Tobacco Smoke (ETS) by the cigarette industry – were sponsored, and the findings printed in scientific journals distributed to health officials and doctors. A courteous smoking campaign was prepared, with stickers, posters and advertisements, to demonstrate that smokers are polite enough to extinguish their cigarettes if asked to do so. One of the most imaginative initiatives was an indoor-air-quality campaign directed at business travellers, airlines, restaurant owners and office managers. With the help of air-quality and ventilation consultants, scientific research and media presentations to business-travel journalists, the tobacco industry argued that smokers were scapegoats for deficiencies in air quality and air conditioning while the real culprits went unpunished: namely, recycled air in sealed aeroplane cabins; inadequate and badly-serviced ventilation in offices and restaurants; harmful emissions from computer screens and photocopiers. The tobacco industry has tackled the problem of under-aged smoking via an extensive publicity campaign.[8]

Initiatives like these have run in a number of countries. From a strictly communications perspective, tobacco's public relations demonstrates how issues managers must be open to a variety of techniques, especially when creating a programme that is global but which also targets small, influential audiences with less direct messages.

International communications has fed the growth of issues management. Distant organizations must contact distant audiences: corporations enlarge the size and detail of their multinational activities; national governments network as whole continents solidify into free-trading blocks; non-commercial organizations band together on planetary issues like global warming or marine pollution. Communicators tangle with cultural and national differences as new arguments, perspectives and methods of doing business are transmitted from one country to another. Two generations ago, the feelings of local inhabitants would not have been a matter of concern for intruding foreign energy companies. Their job was to extract the oil, to sell it and to make a profit. Oil executives preferred to accommodate and often influence the central governments in the affected territories. They failed to communicate effectively to the remainder of the population, other than through technical training and education, and in the end many countries cast aside their rulers and took the oil installations for themselves – with mixed results.

Oil companies were among the first multinational corporations, and among the first to realize that international issues management must be integrated into their global operations. Big oil, with large budgets at its disposal, and with the international character of its work, has absorbed many lessons on the management and mismanagement of worldwide issues. It is not necessary to study the developing world to see international issues management at work, for it has now become important in western countries. There, too, communities are more sensitive to industry than in former days, tend to ask more probing questions than they once asked, and hold the power to disrupt corporate strategy. Lasmo was aware of all this in mid-1989 when it made plans to extract oil off the Atlantic coast of western Nova Scotia and in one of the world's most important fishing grounds. A previous bid for permission to drill had been made by a larger and traditionally aggressive oil company. The applicant failed after its representatives arrived to push the claim. According to a leading regional newspaper, the visitors 'often managed to sound like city slickers trying to tell the provincial hicks down here what was good for them'.[9] In 1988, the Nova Scotian and Canadian governments denied the application, and agreed to a moratorium on drilling into George's Bank until the year 2000. The Bank lay within 500 nautical kilometres of Cohasset and Panuke, the two fields Lasmo wished to develop. Furthermore, the impact of the recent and massive Exxon Valdez oil spill off Alaska loomed large in Nova Scotian considerations. Lasmo, a British company, needed to tackle two important issues: a sensitive population already bruised by an insensitive oil giant and a complete lack of local experience and contacts. Permission to drill would hinge on effective communications. Lasmo decided to engage a Nova Scotian public-affairs consultancy, McArthur Thompson & Law (MTL).

In partnership, the two built a sensitive communications programme, beginning with careful research. On top of the bad blood left by the failed bid, the Exxon Valdez tragedy, and a massive struggle to extract oil from Newfoundland's nearby waters, opinion surveys at that time showed that the environment was a priority among Canadians. According to a consultancy report, 'respondents believed government involvement in environmental issues is necessary and that over one-third of respondents had little confidence in oil companies'.[10] A review was also made of published material on George's Bank. The independent fishermen had united with commercial fishing companies to oppose the George's Bank project, on the grounds that the Bank's stocks were vulnerable to damage from oil exploration. Alliances were sealed with other North American pressure groups fighting similar battles. The oil company eventually responded by opening information centres to the public, but its opponents had already founded NORIG (No Rigs on George's Bank) and exploited their local knowledge and influence. 'We have a responsibility to understand the risk. Our understanding is that we are against it until we know more about it,' said a NORIG spokesman.[11] 'We have witnessed', remarked an observer, 'a virtually unprecedented united front of fishing interests.'[12] 'There is probably not a politician in the province, at any level, whose political future does not depend to some degree on fishing interests,' Lasmo was warned.[13] The George's Bank oil bidders failed to understand the importance of the fisheries. Six thousand people in western Nova Scotia and twenty-five thousand in the province as a whole were directly employed in fishing, with a greater pool of indirect dependants including families and retailers. The fishing business, a Government minister noted, 'contributes approximately one billion dollars to the province'.

By failing to communicate with this rarely-united industry, the company, fatally for its plans, 'created unity where none was possible before'. Instead of dialogue, it ran its own tests on the effects of oil and mud spills on scallop stocks, and held an expensive dinner to seek the views and advice of about fifty select local industrialists and politicians along with the applicant's top executives. This exclusive affair did not go well. The invitees were chosen as likely supporters of the scheme, but the public-affairs efforts of NORIG had not been in vain. A guest recalled he had been 'amazed by the extent of the non-support' among diners for the company's plans, although it was pointed out to them that over 300,000 wells had been drilled worldwide without harm to fisheries. Worse still, the company's main spokesman apparently 'delivered a "Rotary-type" speech as if he was speaking to a group of country hicks'. Undoubtedly, the guest added, this helped spark 'harsh words' between guests and hosts. 'All the company received was more opposition, and this time from an extremely influential, broadly-based, largely business audience.' The firm had made little effort to listen. Information, not dialogue, characterized its efforts. Company information centres, the responses to NORIG through the media, the ill-conceived dinner, and the environmental tests conducted for the company and by the company had sent a pre-packaged and uncompromising message to key provincial publics. A powerful portion of that audience preferred to worry about the living it already made rather than focus on the advantages of striking oil. It was not in a receptive mood, and was suspicious about the capacity of outsiders to decide what was good for it.

By the time that the firm came around to the idea of actually meeting the objectors, the cards and the key influencers were all in NORIG's hands. Under these circumstances, the provincial and federal decision to prevent drilling was inevitable. It was introduced, said the provincial Energy Minister, to 'protect our valuable fishing resource'. Meanwhile, the Nova Scotian Premier visited adjoining New England states and secured an agreement that local governors would lobby Congress to continue its own 'year-by-year moratorium on drilling on the US side of the bank'. 'The George Bank', Premier Buchanan pronounced, 'represents the richest fishery in the world and it must be protected now and for future generations.'[14]

A respected corporation, with many successful and safe drilling projects to its name and with millions to invest in a shaky regional economy, spent a sum estimated at $2 million to start exploration on George's Bank. However, its communications strategy was misguided, failed to win permission to drill, and united business and local communities into an anti-oil coalition too strong and noisy for elected politicians to ignore. On the face of it there seemed little hope for future applications. 'We're not interested in talking about access [to fishing grounds]. We're not interested in talking about insurance payments. We want to fish,' said a NORIG official.[15] NORIG had managed the issue magnificently drawing politicians and media on to its side well before its opponent awoke to the danger. Toward the end of the George's Bank affair, the company was reduced to requesting a public hearing on the issue – often, ironically, the last resort of citizens' groups campaigning *against* projects of this sort.

The legacy of George's Bank meant Lasmo's bid application had to be prepared with extreme care. The standard procedures were all involved, beginning with research: quantitative – the number-crunching of mass opinion surveys of public attitudes on the general issues; and qualitative – personal meetings exploring Lasmo's plans, with specialists and potentially influential figures from 'academia, government, the larger commercial fishery, the independent fishery, the media, the oil industry and the environmental lobby'.[16] The prevailing opinion was that while Lasmo's Panuke and Cohasset fields were not as valuable fisheries as George's Bank, they were regarded by some fishermen as a spawning ground. With overall fish stocks in decline, any threat to that 'nursery' could be strongly opposed. Even tiny oil spills damaged fish catches, and NORIG was alert to the high cost of health scares after recent deaths from the consumption of toxin-impregnated mussels. It was also possible that NORIG's leaders, emboldened by their success, might search for another fight to keep their organization alive.

One 'positive note' revealed by research was the probable attitude of the media. It had been mis-predicting oil in the region for almost a decade, and the constant disappointments affected its approach to the topic. By the time Lasmo arrived on the scene, newspapers were decidedly reluctant to run stories about the imminent arrival of Nova Scotian oil. As a result, the MTL consultants predicted the media were unlikely to show an early interest in the new plans, allowing Lasmo precious time to take its first communications steps away from the spotlight. Once coverage began, the task would be to keep the story 'an oil industry story and not an environmental or fishery story'. 'It will be very difficult to proceed expeditiously with development' noted MTL, 'if we are characterized in the media as posing a threat to the fishery or the environment'.[17] The impact of media mishandling had been felt during the George's Bank application. Nova Scotia's leading newspaper had ignored the oil company's executives on the spot and ran a story suggesting that the corporation's entire Canadian subsidiary was in danger if George's Bank failed. The reason was a massive fine on the American parent company for 'alleged interference' during a take-over bid.[18] Such matters, prominently headlined, were hardly likely to raise expectations that the application for George's Bank would be marked by fair play, trust or openness. In fact, George's Bank had been handled so disastrously it had assumed the character of an exception, blackening the failed corporation so exclusively that little of the mud missed it and spattered over the oil industry in general.

Three other valuable considerations emerged from MTL's investigation. First, the Canadian Petroleum Association (CPA) had already established good relations with the fishing industry; talking with communities in areas affected by oil operations, including Nova Scotia, where it had created a great deal of goodwill. Early in the campaign, several insiders made it clear to Lasmo that the George's Bank bidders 'made a "terrible error" by not participating in CPA and drawing upon this goodwill'. Secondly, the failed bid oversold the benefits, raising expectations and intensifying fears, then dashing expectations under pressure. Last, the failed applicant patronized the fishermen by resorting to clumsy reassurance that everything would be fine. The fishermen believed they knew more about fish stocks.

For Lasmo two years later, the challenge was that the impressions left by George's Bank threatened its own objectives. Added to this was the recent failure of a Chicago-based firm to build local support for a proposed gypsum-loading plant in Halifax, the province's capital. Again, bad communications were felt by some observers to explain the failure, rather than the actual project's substance. There was a prevailing suspicion of proposals and plans laid by 'outsiders', but if communication was the problem, the situation was retrievable. If Lasmo's case was sound, and it was willing to learn from the mistakes of others, a sensitively prepared initiative might have a beneficial influence. Aside from the disastrous dinner, the George's Bank applicant used the press to present its main views. There had been minimal contact between it and NORIG. MTL argued for a dialogue with NORIG ahead of the actual application and its public hearings. 'One way to position ourselves, is to engage now in frank, open-minded discussion with fishing interests with the hope of agreeing on a compensation plan fair to both parties.'[19] MTL warned, 'that there is some urgency to initiating these discussions. Fishing interests will not regard negotiations as being sincere if they are being held simultaneously with a development application being moved through the bureaucracy.'[20] Note the importance of avoiding rather than attracting media coverage – not because Lasmo felt it had anything to hide, but because it understood that the media's ability to create extra 'noise' would distract the company from its honourable attempt to establish open and informed dialogue with fishing-industry representatives, government, and local industry.

The consultancy and Lasmo decided to avoid displaying a 'corporate' face in its communications with the Nova Scotians; 'slick public information programs and tools', were dropped in favour of 'face-to-face discussions wherever possible and materials which were professional and effective without being seen to be extravagant. We limited client exposure at large public meetings in favor of small, carefully targeted audiences.'[21] 'The key people, the so-called opinion leaders, will not be satisfied by glossy brochures or expensive videos alone,' continued the consultancy assessment. 'Rather, they are looking for a sincere commitment to solving problems in a mutually satisfactory way.'[22] Significantly, MTL recommended a concrete demonstration of corporate responsibility, vindicating Ivy Lee's belief that public relations, in order to succeed among informed and intelligent audiences, cannot simply act as a mouthpiece on behalf of others, but must if necessary have a direct role in deciding company policy. 'In a very short order these discussions will lead to the subject of a compensation plan.' If Lasmo would not agree to one, the Government would force one upon them, and in the process undermine public trust in the extent of Lasmo's sincerity. 'We should', argued the consultancy, 'step forward at the outset and initiate negotiations. We don't want to be seen as having to be forced to do what is right.'[23] Final success depended 'on project decisions more than on initiatives of your public relations group'.[24] Lasmo was further advised that the best time to begin communicating on any issue is before it breaks: 'for these negotiations to be seen as an honest effort on the part of the company, they must be held at a time when the other side does not feel they are pressured'.[25] Once an issue becomes public knowledge, the organization primarily involved finds it hard, even impossible, to shape the debate. 'If they [NORIG's representatives] sense undue pressure from us,' noted the consultancy, 'they will be encouraged to cease the negotiations in favor of a more direct appeal to the politicians and Nova Scotians at large'.[26]

The Lasmo team concluded that they could succeed if it was successfully communicated that their plans were modest, 'environmentally benign', and in capable hands; and if they managed to negotiate with the fishing community. In fact, the Lasmo team made efforts to take the 'public' out of its own public relations. No public announcements were made, no applications filed for public hearings. Lasmo even decided – and this is another argument for the need for public relations to reach into wider areas of company policy if need be – not to discuss the application schedule with the news media, and to indicate that it depended on the review process. To have neglected this path would have shown the fishing industry that Lasmo was not taking the negotiations seriously. Precautionary media training was provided, and a recommendation was made to substitute the heated atmosphere of press conferences with one-on-one interviews in the event of approaches from journalists. Brochures were prepared, with careful attention paid to their design: plain, not suspiciously glossy, and 'serious', explaining in some detail the difference between light oil (for which Lasmo was drilling), and heavy oil – the sort people think about when they think of oil slicks.

Over-eager public-relations practitioners often confuse their role in presenting company policy, mistaking it for an ability to represent the company on all crucial occasions. In issues management as in all non-marketing matters, it is usually far better to put the leaders of the company themselves in front of the key audiences. MTL and Lasmo avoided this trap. From summer 1989 to spring 1990 its own executives met privately 'with fishery and environmental groups and with government officials, at both political and bureaucratic levels'.[27] Four key messages were prepared in advance, and formed the core of Lasmo's discussions. They were simple, and addressed the concerns of the fishing community:

1. Oil from Cohasset and Panuke is extremely light, having the consistency and colour of a cup of weak tea.

2. The production area is not heavily fished, is ice free and the seas are relatively calm.

3. Lasmo's project is not a 'mega-project'. It is small, costing less than 5 per cent of the estimated costs for the Hibernia development planned for the North Atlantic off Newfoundland.

4. The production technology for this project has been successfully used the world over; no technological innovations are required.

Unusually, but wisely, the regional benefits of the project were presented in a modest light to audiences who already had livings of their own and were likely to react against the environmental implications of a large development. Lasmo's forecast for the scheme was subdued: 'The Cohasset/Panuke development is small compared to other projects proposed for the East Coast offshore,' stated the company. Its impact would be 'helpful' to the Province, and present 'Nova Scotians with an excellent opportunity to expand knowledge and skills in offshore'.[28] Lasmo also managed to retain NORIG's second-in-command as its main spokesperson. Such public endorsement from a prominent opponent of the previous project was persuasive, and a sign of the credibility Lasmo had managed to establish among Nova Scotian opinion leaders. Following a series of private meetings, the company felt ready to submit its application to public hearings by the spring of 1990. The region's media were officially brought 'into the loop', contacted for the names of the reporters covering the hearings, and supplied with names of Lasmo personnel, and advance information on the project. When media coverage appeared, the tone was optimistic, mingled perhaps with relief after a decade of failed predictions: 'N.S. [Nova Scotia's] offshore oil's small-scale, but coming.'[29] 'Lasmo going the distance.'[30] 'Oil company predicts N.S. oil spill to have "minor" effect on fishery.'[31]

Lasmo's application to produce oil was approved by the Canada–Nova Scotia Offshore Petroleum Board in September 1990. It was Canada's first offshore oil production platform. Lasmo's issues management team followed up this success with careful monitoring, but ultimately was able to say that 'no organised opposition to the project emerged over the eighteen months of Lasmo operations in the province'.[32] The oil came onshore in 1992.

NOTES

1 Thatcher, Margaret. *The Downing Street Years*. (New York: HarperCollins, 1993) p287.
2 'The classless society'. *The Economist*, 19 February 1994, pp 61–2.
3 BBC2. *Public Eye*. 8–8.30pm, 3 June 1994.
4 Ibid.
5 A detailed identification of 'eight kinds of publics defined by the three independent variables of the Grunig theory of communication behaviour', explores levels of audience involvement and commitment in Grunig, J. and Hunt, T., *Managing Public Relations* (New York: Holt, Rinehart & Winston (USA), 1984) p 153.
6 'The killer we don't discuss'. *Newsweek*, 27 December 1993, p 40.
7 See, for example: http://www.idiom.com/bilofsky/astrotrf.htm. The World Wide Web is energetically debating this issue.
8 For example: 'Is Your Building Sick?' *PR Newswire*, New York, 23 July 1987. To: Healthcare and science editors.
9 'Steps towards success'. *Halifax Herald*, Saturday, 4 August 1990.
10 IPRA Golden World Entry, 1991. 'McArthur, Thompson & Law. "Winning Environmental Approval for Canada's First Offshore Oil Project." Halifax, Nova Scotia, Canada'. Project Summary, p 1.
11 'Texaco surveying on George's Bank'. *Chronicle–Herald*, 12 August 1987.
12 IPRA Golden World Entry, 1991. 'McArthur, Thompson & Law'.
13 Ibid. 'Research'. Opinion Research, p 3.
14 Press release from the Office of the Premier. 15 June 1988.
15 'George's Bank drilling uncertainty causing problems'. *Chronicle–Herald*, 4 March 1988.

16 IPRA Golden World Entry, 1991. 'McArthur Thompson & Law'. Project Summary, p 1.

17 Ibid., 'Research'. News Media.

18 *Chronicle–Herald*, 10 March 1988.

19 IPRA Golden World Entry, 1991. 'McArthur, Thompson & Law'. Planning & Strategy. 'Strategic Communications Plan', Recommendation 1.

20 Ibid., Recommendation 2.

21 Ibid., 'Planning'.

22 Ibid., 'Research'. Discussion, p 1.

23 Ibid., 'Social/Political Assessment', 12 September 1989, p 2.

24 Ibid., 'Discussion'. p 3.

25 Ibid., 'Social/Political Assessment', 12 September 1989. p 2.

26 Ibid.

27 Ibid., 'Project Summary', p 3.

28 Lasmo Nova Scotia Limited. *Folder: Cohasset/Panuke Development*. 'Opportunities' file.

29 *Sunday Daily News*, 26 January 1990.

30 *Port of Halifax Newsletter*, Spring 1990.

31 *Chronicle–Herald*, 26 March 1990.

32 IPRA Golden World Entry, 1991. Project Summary, p 3.

CHAPTER SEVEN

Fear, and the Death of Communications

I realised I had lost my way and that countless
difficulties lay in wait for me before I found my
way home . . . I told myself that I should be resolute
and make a quick decision. The day was passing, and
soon mysterious darkness would descend.[1]

Naguib Mafouz

Issues management is when an organization communicates about a range of external matters affecting the success of its operations. Risk communications is possibly its most lively, dramatic and distinctive manifestation. It is when organizations must respond to persistent audience perceptions that their operations or products are a direct, physical, threat to human life and limb.

Risk communications, and its volatile variant of crisis communications, is the most concentrated and exciting form of issues management. In crises, the communications managers of corporations whose chemicals have leaked or exploded, whose tanker has spilled crude oil, whose product has been tampered with, are not at all concerned with increasing the amount of publicity the corporation receives. They are more interested in trying to clamp some controls upon the anarchy: is the company being open, or giving the impression of insecurity by dodging difficult questions? Is it doing anything to help the victims and potential victims, the nervous shareholders and angry politicians? Is it showing that it is trying to discover what happened and who was responsible? Is it big enough to say it is sorry, and if need be even withdraw the product? Is the crisis management team taking control of the communications agenda in a responsible way, with a credible system for handling media and public enquiries? Are the corporation's leaders disciplined enough to respond in all these ways under the most extreme pressures, brave enough to face the world when they most wish they could hide from it? Survival hinges on careful communications delivered at speed: sending out visible signs that the corporation is doing its best, and is doing it competently and responsibly. Prudent organizations create 'preparedness manuals', identifying key audiences in advance, preparing likely answers to likely questions, setting down the public-relations procedures with the fire-drill clarity required in times of panic. Less prudent organizations do not.

Risk communications can drag out over a longer period. Is Mexican-grown food dangerous? CNN, the highly influential news station, prepared a special report exploring that possibility. The reporter begins his story at a border crossing. He asks whether the large volumes of Mexican food, freely crossing the border as a result of the North American Free Trade Agreement (NAFTA), have been sufficiently checked for pesticide content by over-worked customs officials.[2] We are then informed that the Mexican government admits it is unable to control the way in which pesticides are used by Mexican farmers. Worse, analysis of raw sewage overflows from Mexico into San Diego in the US has detected DDT, a banned pesticide in Mexico and the United States. Fred Williamson, a representative for a large Mexican farming concern now appears on screen: 'I've heard DDT forever', he complains, as workers toil in the field behind him, 'and it's not true. It's just flat not true, but it sounds good.'[3] 'All that will now be reassessed,' concludes the reporter, back in the studio and facing the camera. Note the 'now'. Evidently the reporter feels he has introduced new fizz to the debate. So he has. Whether the DDT stories are true is not the issue. Whether the amount of actual DDT found is truly dangerous is not the issue. The issue is that viewers are probably familiar with the name 'DDT', that they will not relish the prospect of finding it in their food or water. Fear is irrational, and fears of poisoned water and food number among the most fundamental manifestations of irrationality, added to fear of being at the mercy of an unregulated and disorganized foreign country. The problem is 'now' that viewers may feel they are threatened, and that the interviewed farmer was hiding the truth from them (it does not matter that the farmer himself is observing the law: it is doubtful whether any of the lawbreakers would volunteer to be interviewed).

It is a safe bet that, as these uncompromising denials continue, the search for alternative views will intensify; maybe over months, maybe over years, until the people perceived to be responsible – the Mexican government and farmers – are no longer trusted, and find themselves at the receiving end of popular, media-backed political action over which they will have little control. Mexican food marketers have not, at the time of writing, made an obvious adjustment to incorporate a demonstrable, active, public acknowledgement of the pesticide risk into their communications. They are opting for a policy of denial. They feel defensive because they feel under attack. By not facing the matter head on, their arguments are unheard; but as the tobacco industry and many others have discovered, the publicity will continue without the benefit of their input, probably to the advantage of their competitors.[4]

The same day, another channel carries a report on the aftermath, fifteen years on, of the 1979 leak from the Three Mile Island nuclear power plant in New Jersey. It reveals that above-average cancer rates are still at large in the area where the disaster originally occurred, and describes incidents that local people suspect are a long-term legacy of the leak. The reporter mentions the 'high number' of aborted farm animals, and talks with residents suffering from various cancers and who have lost children in childbirth. Jeb Wilson, a careful lawyer representing the owners of Three Mile Island, is also interviewed. Here is the section of his interview that was actually shown:

> Lots of these people are suing because they genuinely don't know, and they think maybe the accident had something to do with it, and maybe this lawsuit might give them more information about that.[5]

Cut to Debbie Baker, who has organized Red Alert, a group of thirty homes around the plant where concerned mothers monitor radiation levels using a hand-held device. She expresses her view of the corporation's tactics: 'Each time an occurrence has happened, they've always paid money as opposed to finding out the answers.' However well intentioned the corporation's lawyer, his message as it appeared on screen is not liable to win much public understanding. He only seemed to speak about the victims' motives, without expressing sympathy for their suffering. Corporations under such pressures often shy away from sympathy on the grounds that it might legally incriminate them. Yet not to publicly express sympathy can also incriminate them in the minds and actions of the public who decide their commercial fate.

Risk communications is as much about nudging a frightened organization into facing its publics as it is about encouraging those publics to put their trust in a besieged organization. It is a subtle and sensitive business, a significant branch of public-relations practice, and demonstrates how structured communications can re-establish acceptance and dialogue in unfavourable circumstances. Risks are steamrollers. They appear on the horizon, distant enough for an organization to pretend they are not really there, to try to forget about it. The steamroller may take years to arrive, but the closer it gets the harder it is to shrug off institutional paralysis and step away from its crushing wheel. Crises are roller coasters, risks compressed into days or hours. They can break out overnight and are resolved by the speed with which the organization responds; its openness and sincerity. Risk and crisis communications can retrieve organizations from the path of slow or instant destruction. They must deal sensitively with human nature in a vulnerable and emotional condition. They must close the ground between the risk-takers and the audiences who view themselves as possible future victims. Psychological research conducted in the United States has exposed the breadth of the communications gap between risk-carriers and their publics by demonstrating gulfs in perceptions, approach and language.[6]

On one side of the gap is frequency and on the other tendencies. Tendencies boil a risk down into fractions, reducing it to a point where it no longer feels threatening to the morale and the morals of the risk-carrying organization, and in the process it ceases to be seen as a communications priority. But for a concerned citizen, politician or investigative reporter, it is the frequencies that matter, the impulse to see the threat in integers – whole numbers, or a whole person. For example, a reporter will describe the slow deaths of the Japanese mercury-poison victims at Minamata. A harassed communications executive in company headquarters is less ready to confront his company's safety record in this way. He finds it easier to survive tragedy by calculating the risk percentage per person in all communities where his plants are located. He might prefer to think of, say, the 0.0002 per cent chance of contamination per person nationwide, rather than lie in bed at night remembering the televised faces of the high percentage of individual sufferers in an affected locality. This is an important consideration for public relations, as psychologists have concluded that 'presentation format is important'.[7]

> The precise manner in which risks are expressed can have a major impact on perceptions and behaviour. For example, an action increasing one's annual chances of death from 1 in 10,000 to 1.3 in 10,000 would probably be seen as much more risky if it were described, instead, as producing a 30% increase in annual mortality risk.[8]

Risk communicators must be sensitive to frequencies, because they are the starting position for their critical audiences. They must also be sensitive to the irrational, decisive power of emotion when audiences confronting risks are choosing who to believe and deciding how scared they should feel:

> one can present people with two choices that, in terms of formal logic, are equivalent – yet one choice may be strongly and consistently preferred and may carry an emotional weight altogether different from that of the other choice. On the other hand, one can offer people two logically disparate choices, yet the people may see them as equivalent.[9]

There is a logical equivalence between a pure water supply containing no DDT, and a pure water supply that might contain minute traces of DDT. In both cases, the water is unaffected by the DDT. Given the choice of these two equivalents, which one will be preferred by San Diego house-holders? Is their choice guided by logic or emotion? Is that choice potentially likely to influence the American authorities in their own atti-tude towards Mexican food production? How will the Mexican food producers respond? Evidence suggests that besieged organizations, tightly bound by strong existing lines of seniority and task-responsibility, find irrationality hard to incorporate into their daily rhythm. They may respond to the prospect of emotion-led risk by opting out, by choosing not to communicate. But they cannot stop normally reliable supporters from forming their own impressions, exclusively drawn from other, less friendly, sources.

One consequence of the intensity of modern communications is that it opens choice and destroys automatic loyalties. People are more exposed to competing messages. More choice, less loyalty. More forgetfulness due to the alternative information we have available. In these circumstances, the impact of silence on an audience can be marked. Years of silence between a company and the media, local residents, politicians or even – in extreme cases – its employees, can be positively perilous and perilously permanent. The 'death' of communications guarantees two other developments. It guarantees a withdrawal of trust. Local residents feel insecure about a nearby chemical firm because it refuses to accept responsibility for mysterious and persistent emissions and spillages. Risks creep out from unexpected sources. A respected carpet company with an excellent tradition of customer relations fails to respond to revelations that many carpets are imported from manufacturers on the Asian subcontinent who employ underfed, abused and poverty-stricken children. When the South Asian Coalition on Child Servitude completes a protest march across India and calls on western consumers to boycott goods produced by India's 55 million exploited children, the company suddenly finds itself in the public eye.[10] British cattle, after centuries of careful breeding, are traditionally the best foundation for any beef herd in the world. However, the trust of generations of consumers and overseas farmers evaporates in a few years because of the fear that BSE – or mad cow disease – might be passed on, fatally, to human consumers of infected British-bred cattle. British agriculturists attempt simple denial, then – when anxious humans continue to worry about contamination – scramble to repair the damage with a frantic communications campaign of their own. But the surge in critical publicity is too strong. Import bans are introduced by trading partners overseas, threatening the existence of an established business and the breeders, markets and shippers involved in it. The final sign of a withdrawal of trust in a corporation is a refusal to believe in its communications.

When trust is sucked out from the existing communications between an organization and its publics, belief goes with it. The longer belief is suspended, the less likely it is to be restored. The quicker and more openly an organization responds, the easier the task of recovery. Belief depends on the feeling that, as with Lasmo in Nova Scotia, an organization is being open with its audiences, that it is not hiding bitter truths however damaging they are to the organization itself. It has already been said that denial feels safer, and the observation deserves closer attention. The urge to push a looming threat to one side is entirely natural, especially among middle managers planning for the short term – but a series of good short terms does not always equal an excellent long term. If denial affects part of the organism, it is quite likely to spread elsewhere. Others tacitly, or openly, co-operate in the suppression of distasteful truths and focus solely upon their routine tasks. In 1945, the staff in Hitler's bunker continued denying the collapse taking place around them even as the Soviets fought their way into Berlin. 'I had a name for this unreal world of the bunker,' recalled one witness. 'I called it the Isle of the Departed . . . [because] . . . the apparatus of command continued to run mechanically. Apparently there was still some momentum here which went on operating even when the motor was running down.'[11] This vivid memory captures the essence of risk-denial in any sort of organization. Language, ideals and behaviour adapt to incorporate denial into daily work, and inexorably into a corporation's public identity. The final effect of short-term denial is an irreversible public conviction that the organization is unethical, and a withdrawal of belief in it by media, customers, shareholders and regulatory agencies.

The fate of asbestos, recounted by a former executive in one of that industry's top companies, demonstrates the destructive effects of risk-denial and the avoidance of communications:

> Had the company responded to the dangers of asbestosis and lung cancer with extensive medical research, assiduous communication, insistent warnings, and a rigorous dust-reduction program, it could have saved lives and would probably have saved the stockholders, the industry, and, for that matter, the product.[12]

It was, argues Bill Sells in his enlightening essay, 'one of the most colossal corporate blunders of the twentieth century'.[13] Generations of asbestos executives preferred to deny the accumulating weight of medical evidence, which first appeared at the turn of the twentieth century and expanded with increasing incidents of asbestos-linked lung cancer. The industry quietly established a trust fund for the victims. It refused to raise the issue with sceptical customers. It took a partisan stance by conducting and attempting to publicize its own scientific research. Too late, it initiated proper dust-reduction procedures in the workplace. It took refuge in proclamations that it was observing the letter of the law – a classic posture adopted by companies locked into denial – and gave no sign that it cared enough to exceed the letter of the law and display a personal commitment to rectifying the matter. It cast around for other guilty parties. It tried picking on the tobacco industry on the grounds that cigarette-smoking asbestos workers were at even greater risk of lung cancer. Tobacco companies, in their turn, were later to attack poor ventilation and maintenance as the main contributor to unhealthy indoor air. The problem for asbestos was that tobacco already acknowledged the risk in its warning labels on packs; asbestos could not steel itself to do the same. It left itself exposed to critics by sacrificing long-term belief to short-term denial. Starved of customers, and rupturing under the burden of massive settlements, the once blue-chip asbestos business had largely expired by the 1980s. Sells believes asbestos did not expire because the product was uniquely dangerous. He notes that many organizations continue to manufacture and profit from hazardous chemicals. Rather asbestos was killed by a refusal to face the facts, and a related failure to communicate them persuasively. So ineffective had it been and so guilty did it seem, that even after the industry's death, claims against it from victims and putative victims continued to increase. By the 1990s, personal injury lawsuits claiming asbestos damage had reached six figures, clogging up the arteries of the American judicial system.

By virtue of planning and patience, it is possible to prise open an organization – or a person – and help it to face its greatest fear calmly and openly. That achieved, it becomes possible to channel the risk into a constructive communications programme. Some observations on political leadership made by Helmut Schmidt, the former West German Chancellor, vindicate the open approach to risk:

> Often enough, you cannot convince the people to do something that they find very unpopular. The only chance you have is for them to know you as a dependable person of judgement. If they have confidence in you, which they can only acquire by experience, then they might be willing to follow you even if you take some unpopular moves. You can, in the course of such a chain of events, even build your popularity on doing unpopular things.[14]

As with politicians, so also with organizations. The greater the respect for an organization, the broader the public tolerance of its activities. The key is open communication. Politicians are highly aware of this. They know that their profession occasionally carries risks: of policy failure; above all, the risk of losing public support. Company executives are not elected, and even those working in industries where, unlike politics, the risk is perpetual and obvious are often surprisingly unaware of their own communications vulnerability. In northern Europe, an official corporation responsible for disposing of its country's hazardous waste faced serious criticism from environmentalists, and from residents in the vicinity of its main incineration plant. A public campaign against it ran unopposed for five years, complete with demonstrations, publicized scientific surveys, petitions, and the advantages of building up, unopposed, strong media contacts. In all that time, the waste company made no attempt to communicate. They failed to appoint communications experts to act for them. They ignored the appointment of a leading green activist to the position of environment minister. Finally, when the company formally proposed an extension to its plant, it handed its opponents an excellent publicity opportunity. Executives found themselves obliged to justify their action to a large, outraged, influential and disbelieving audience. Eventually, they decided to retain a communications consultancy, which nudged them towards accepting openness and dialogue. The first step was to 'demystify' the management of waste. Local residents were invited to visit the plant and responded in large numbers; a regular newsletter about the site and about hazardous waste was produced and distributed to neighbourhoods and opinion leaders including administrators, politicians and journalists. Journalists used the newsletter, ran stories on it and were given to understand that they would at last be able to obtain comment from the once-taciturn corporation.

We have concentrated so far on the need for organizations to convey concern about risks, and to demonstrate an unswerving commitment to tackling them. Trust and belief also respond to objectivity. Risk communications is emphatically not about putting an organization's 'spin' on a problem. Cancer sufferers on Three Mile Island do not really want to know the corporation's medical view on what might really be responsible for their plight, however sound the evidence. If research papers are sponsored by Mexican food growers to prove that their produce is safe from pesticides, journalists are unlikely to accept the results as uncritically as the sponsors. The most sincere and balanced research, as Sells later found when he backed an investigation that concluded that his fibre-glass was not carcinogenic, is treated as biased if the media and government feel that the source has a partisan interest. 'We should have involved the regulators,' he realized. 'A negative finding that was based on their own assumptions would have been more difficult for them to pick apart.'[15] Customers and shareholders must likewise be convinced that the company is being open with them, and dispassionately addressing the risk. The media must be encouraged to respect the company as an accessible, knowledgeable and conscientious communicator. Competitors must be monitored for unfair claims or criticism.

A risk is not always the fault of the corporation it damages. Some organizations find themselves shouldering responsibility for wider social problems. The Canadian branch of the International Council of Shopping Centres (ICSC) took the pulse of its customers after media reports started to link teenage gangs, prostitution and drug dealing to shopping malls.[16] One parent commented: 'The concern we have with malls is that the kids are going to get kidnapped.' Another agreed: 'That's right – you turn your back and they're gone.'[17] How simple it would be if tendencies could be applied, and the ICSC merely had to state the infinitesimal odds against kidnapping. But fear is frequential. It works in whole numbers, the whole number in this case being the parent's son or daughter under threat by entering a mall. To stress the infinitesimal odds against individual harm would not come close to reassuring parents: it might even appear callous. Inappropriate risk communications, missing the target with the wrong message, would not prevent shoppers from withdrawing their trust, belief and patronage of shopping centres. One parent remarked: 'I'm not happy that they [the children] like to go to the mall because they're not going shopping. It is a sort of entertainment.'[18] The ICSS, which represents 29,000 mall retailers and operators in 42 countries, resisted risk-denial and instead prepared 'Kids Sense', an activity programme in Canada designed to address the issue openly at an early stage, by communicating its members' concern and commitment.

The 1991 'Kids Sense' outstripped its predecessors in scale. It started researching the fears and the proposals of parents themselves. The concerns were tabulated: parents were sceptical about the commitment of mall management to their children's safety. They were, in the tradition of people who feel at risk from an organization, suspicious of mall management's motives for getting involved with such serious issues. Malls were felt to be suitable places for certain kinds of safety demonstrations. Street safety, bike safety, self-defence were fine, a participative programme involving give-aways was preferred, but 'more serious topics' such as drugs, alcohol and tobacco were perceived as the province of proper experts working from more authoritative surroundings – in schools or the home. In other words, the issues parents thought were unfitted for mall programmes, were those that the malls actually wanted to tackle. Drugs and alcohol were more likely dangers in a mall than bike or swimming accidents but, irrationally, parents concentrated on the latter. 'Kids Sense' was thereupon widened to tackle the preferred issues of bicycle and tricycle safety, and fire prevention, and wove the ICSC's specific concerns into a 'street proofing' initiative aimed at helping lost or hassled children. Meanwhile, parents remained suspicious about the credibility of malls as promoters of safety. The ICSC therefore decided to launch the programme in partnership with the YMCA, responsible for the largest child-care programme in Canada. Local police officers and firefighters participated in three days of safety-awareness presentations involving balloons, puppet shows, clowns and colouring books.

The virtue of 'Kids Sense' was driven home by a letter of support from Canada's Governor-General, and by switching the 1991 programme (away from the gathering gloom of October) to the longer days of May, on the verge of the summer vacation. As a trade association, the ICSC could advise and encourage, but not compel, its members to partake of Kid's Sense. A detailed package was assembled to prod them out of denial into action. Local malls were sent a detailed outline programme to adopt and adapt, even down to sample news releases alerting local media to the activities. Handouts and posters were prepared and distributed, and a national search launched for a child 'Safety Hero'. Over 290 shopping centres chose to host the programme. The stories of all the regional nominees and the two who finally received national awards attracted considerable local and national media coverage.

NOTES

1 Mafouz, Naguib. 'The conjuror made off with the dish', *The Time, the Place, and Other Stories* (New York: Doubleday, 1992) p 23.
2 CNN. Morning News. 'Food and Health', 24 March 1994.
3 Ibid.
4 See, for example, 'In our children's food'. *Frontline*, with Bill Moyers. PBS TV. 19 April 1994, 9–10pm. A second, one-hour, investigation into pesticides and food, again with reference to Mexican DDT usage.
5 ABC. 24 March, 1994.
6 Notable work in this area includes: Kahnemann, Daniel; Tversky, Amos; Slovic, Paul. *Judgement under Uncertainty* (Cambridge University Press (USA), 1982). Arkes, Hal R. and Hammond, Kenneth R. (eds). *Judgement and Decision Making* (Cambridge University Press (USA), 1986).
7 Slovic, Paul; Fischoff, Baruch; Lichtenstein, Sarah. 'Facts versus fears: Understanding perceived risk', in Arkes and Hammond, *Judgement and Decision Making*, pp 478–9.
8 Ibid.
9 Sapolsky, Robert M. 'On Human Nature'. *The Sciences*, March/April 1994, p 10.
10 CBC radio. *News* (10am, 11am). 24 April 1994.
11 Speer, Albert. *Inside the Third Reich* (London: Sphere, 1971) pp 630–1.
12 Sells, Bill. 'What asbestos taught me about managing risk'. *Harvard Business Review*, March–April 1994, p 76.
13 Ibid.
14 Webber, Alan M. 'The Statesman as CEO: An interview with Helmut Schmidt'. *Harvard Business Review*, Jul–Aug 1986, p 68.
15 Sells, 'What asbestos taught me', p 88.
16 A good example of media coverage of the problems facing North American malls, and the responses of mall owners, can be found in 'The miracle on Dufferin Street: How a dangerous, decaying, mall was transformed into a vibrant social centre'. *Toronto Star*, Section B, Saturday, 16 April 1994, pp B1 and B4.
17 IPRA Golden World Entry, 1991. 'International Council of Shopping Centers'. 'Kids Sense/Enfants Avertis'. Research.
18 Ibid.

CHAPTER EIGHT

Tin Cans and Temples: Public Relations and the Myths of Power

While thus she spake, the gods that gave good ear
To her bold words, and marked well her grace
. . . stood all astonied; like a sort of steers,
'Mongst whom some beast of strange and foreign race
Unwares is chanced, far straying from his peers;
So did their ghastly gaze bewray their hidden fears.

Spenser: *The Faerie Queene*

PUBLIC RELATIONS: TOOL OF THE POWERFUL

Edmund Spenser's *The Faerie Queene* is a long, famous and poetic tribute dedic-ated to Elizabeth I. It carefully constructs her in the image of an independent-minded, powerful, and magical creature who thumbs her nose at the gods themselves. It is one of the sixteenth century's greatest literary achievements, and in addition a lengthy exercise in image promotion on behalf of a strong woman. The bonds between power and communications have not always been as magnificently realized, especially in the television age, when large masses of less literary people need to be contacted. But the bonds are usually no less intimate. Without communications, power cannot properly assert its authority. Without power, communication is purposeless. As we shall see, this interdependence presents problems for the gods of power. Many of them worry that public relations actually controls and shapes their policies instead of restricting its duties to presentation, and occasionally sucks the real point out of them. Despite this dilemma, ambitious political, commercial and other seekers of power continue exploiting communications to achieve their goals.

That communications can apparently serve up power, loyalty and meaning for anyone or anything is shown by the triumph of that theoretically trivial container of caramelized gloop sold by the billion across planet Earth since the end of World War II. The values embodied by Coca-Cola came to transcend the product itself, and then bore it irresistibly forward. 'The "American Way of Life" (another cliché of the period) was vindicated with every bottle of Coca-Cola sold,' a respected historian of the United States has commented.[1] American presidents were more than ready to lend the soft drink a little of their own authority by imbibing the tradition. Coke's photographers caught Truman, Eisenhower, Kennedy and their successors drinking the product. Fidel Castro, too; for few parts of the world exist where a Coca-Cola can is not instantly recognizable. It is becoming a modern myth; a metaphor for certain political and cultural principles. The arrival of Coke or its equally sticky opponent Pepsi in a country is often seen as a public step towards economic and even political liberation – or domination. In the film *The Gods must be Crazy*, a Coke bottle drops from the sky to affect the lives of perplexed Kalahari bushmen.

How did this fluid win so much authority? As communicators, we must be interested not only in how it originally happened, but in how it has *continued* to happen – for that is where public relations enters the frame. Without putting public relations to work, continuously cultivating the Coca-Cola corporation's public identity, we would have lost that little concoction to history a long time ago. As it stands today, Coca-Cola's achievement is rather remarkable. In the summer of 1985, the attack on its disastrous attempt to alter the flavour paradoxically exposed the strength of its existing hold on the public. According to one account, over five thousand angry calls a day were made to the consumer hotline. Forty thousand letters of protest were written. One writer informed the company that he was rethinking his Will, which decreed that his cremated ashes were to be sealed in a Coke can and buried in Arlington National Cemetery.[2] Extending or defending its public image and reputation is a task of quasi-religious proportions. Executives guard the drink's contents as closely as acolytes protected the Delphic oracle's inner sanctuaries. Coca-Cola is a global product bottling a blend of western, American and 'international' values almost as hard to separate as the drink's ingredients. The sum total of opinions held about Coca-Cola equals its image. The fate of a multimillion dollar organization, thousands of employees and investors, and the willingness of millions of consumers to drink the stuff, hinges upon that image, for that is what they are buying. 'The Coca-Cola Company,' it is written, 'was perhaps the first consumer-focused multinational because it marketed not only a retail product, but values and even lifestyles.'[3]

It has often been argued that 'myths' are vital to our lives. We turn to such tales, and the lessons they sometimes embody, for inward gratification in our passage through the toils and moils of everyday, practical existence. 'The individual', Joseph Campbell believed, 'has to find an aspect of myth that relates to his own life.'[4] In this sense, Coca-Cola embodies a 'myth' that helps us experience and accept the facts about power in our corporate age. The public relations of successful manufactured products like Coke builds from the same emotional foundation, whether resigned or eager and uncritical, that pre-industrial humanity gave to its political and religious rulers. 'There are only two things in my life: God and Coca-Cola. Now you have taken one of those things away from me,' cried another bereft victim of Coke's short-lived flavour change.[5] The very first persons to put detailed, structured communications at the service of their preferred image and will brewed a similar alchemy of religious and personal power. Over three thousand years ago, Pharaoh Rameses II (the Great) built a massive temple to himself at Abu Simbel, decorating it with wall carvings depicting his family abased in worship before him, and Rameses himself glorying in the severed hands and genitals of slaughtered enemies. Public relations today would have had little to teach Rameses. He had, noted an eminent Egyptologist, 'a passion for self-advertisement'.[6] This view is widespread, but a little too general to help us fully comprehend Rameses' intention.

To communications specialists, it is plain that this long-dead ruler was not boasting at random, and that he understood the value of a carefully thought-out public-relations plan. At Abu Simbel, and at sites elsewhere, he was sending a definite message about the image of himself he felt it necessary to portray. Rameses also displayed his talents as a publicist by erecting Abu Simbel at the southern edge of his empire, overlooking the Nile. The temple was not intended for his own people; it was an early exercise in international communications. Rameses' 'key audience' was the potentially hostile Nubians to the south who often travelled downriver for trade or war. As they entered his realm they saw Abu Simbel, carved into the living rock, with four titanic statues of Rameses himself seated at the entrance and glaring over them. We know that in Egypt's Nubian territories Rameses' general policy of self-publicization was at its 'most conspicuous'.[7]

> My name is Ozymandias, king of kings:
> Look upon my works, ye Mighty, and despair![8]

Shelley explored the original intent of this sort of message in his famous reflections upon a later Rameses. If the earlier Rameses was attempting to secure this degree of awe from Egypt's southern neighbours, then Abu Simbel unarguably demonstrates his grasp of the basic principles of public relations: decide upon your message and policy, select your audience, and deliver the message in a form that they are likely to understand and remember. Ivy Lee's simple principle of publicity states:

> Publicity comprises advertising, of course; it comprises the radio, the moving picture, magazine articles, speeches, books, mass meetings, brass bands, parades; everything involved in the expression of an idea or an institution – including the policy or the idea expressed.[9]

The greatest difference between Pharaoh's communications and our own is that, instead of *words* and *momentary images*, relayed by 'moving picture, magazine articles, speeches', he preferred *durable shapes*: temples, statues and poetry, to express an idea about himself. Modern leaders occasionally follow in his footsteps: President Mitterand of France sponsored an important series of public buildings in the historic centre of Paris. A predecessor, President Georges Pompidou, backed the controversial arts centre that bears his name. Ceausescu of Romania erected a 'titanic new palace, a pharaonic pile five years in the making'. 'Nearly half a mile long' but not finished by the time of his execution.[10] Evidently architecture does not need to be finished to send the builder's public-relations message. After all, the temple that impressed Shelley was a 'colossal wreck'. It led him to take a paradoxical position. He was moved by the decay to remark on the vanity of earthly power, and simultaneously inspired enough by it to perpetuate, in the same short poem, the name and works of the temple's owner. That is, perhaps, a tension of opposites that injects his poem with power. Over a century later, the architect Albert Speer was similarly affected by the ruins of imperial Rome. He used his awakening to the message-carrying meaning of wreckage to construct a 'theory of ruin value'. His master Hitler – who generally knew a helpful communications mechanism when he saw one – turned it into an official requirement for all public building projects. Speer's theory decreed that all buildings in the supposed 'Thousand Year Reich' should be constructed with an eye to the impressive, romantic, effect that they would make as ruins in the far-distant future. Incidentally, the public relations value of wreckage today need take us no further than the bombed-out air-raid shelter in Baghdad, filmed by the western television crews that Saddam Hussein's functionaries led there after an American missile attack.

So Rameses the Great did not hesitate to publicize his greatness through architecture, but how truthful is it? Certainly, the popular view is to take him at face value on the evidence of his temples, his proclamations and his obvious overpowering belief in his own greatness. However, historians foraging beyond these visible signs are raising doubts. His historic victory at Kadesh over the Hittites, the one proclaimed in gory detail on the walls at Abu Simbel, may not actually have been a victory after all, but a stand-off, since Rameses withdrew and the Hittites were left in possession of the field. One commentator considers that: 'the length of his reign and his sheer assertiveness made him appear more formidable than is justified by his actual achievements'.[11] Perhaps Rameses' actual achievement is to have launched a public-relations programme that has carried his carefully constructed image of power and strength far into the distant future. However, the manifestations of that message have oddly changed to match our own preoccupations. Yes, Rameses is remembered by us as 'the Great', but his potent name now adorns a top-selling brand of condoms. His monument to slaughter and self-adoration has become a historic treasure. The peace-keepers of the United Nations carefully moved the old warrior's temple away from the rising waters of Lake Nasser. Now protected, its job is to attract revenue from curious holidaymakers, not scare encroaching Nubians into good behaviour. Given the respect that the modern world is paying to Abu Simbel it can be safely said that, all in all, Rameses chose a highly successful medium for his communications.

He chose his message well, too. It appears to have been carefully prepared, and not the passionate whim of an egomaniac. Egypt was recovering from a long period of unrest and decline when Rameses came to power. He or his advisers seem to have realized that long and stable rule from a strong leader was essential. Rameses' key messages may have stemmed not from his conceited view of his own importance, but from a carefully considered policy – as all successful public relations should. His achievements are questionable, yet, for all that, 'the events of his sixty-seven years of reign are better known and present more of interest than those of any other equal span of Egyptian history.'[12]

Powerful people do not always have Rameses' resources at their disposal, and depend on cheaper methods. These have included poems and song. Ancient history records the name of perhaps the first professional communications consultant – possibly the only one for a long time thereafter. In the fifth century BC the Greek poet Simonides placed his poems in the service of publicity, selling songs of praise to wealthy rulers. True to perceptions of public relations today, his career seems generally to have been considered in bad taste. Later Greek writers accused Simonides of greed; apparently his poems were in great demand and attracted high prices. Nevertheless, he was so popular that he had political influence, and his poems on the wars with Persia doubtless gave a powerful impulse to local patriotism.

Simonides had political customers, and public relations has been developed by politicians more than any other group of people. This is not surprising. Helmut Schmidt reminds us that politicians must be especially sensitive to their publics:

> You must be able to convince those whose consensus you need. And you have to use methods of convincing your members of parliament or the electorate quite different from those necessary for a chief executive or an officer of a bank or an industrial corporation. The CEO can just say, 'I want it to be done this way and that way,' and if people don't agree, they get fired. But you can't fire your electorate! It is the other way around here – your electorate fires you. And this happens quite often, much more often than a chief executive is fired by his shareholders.[13]

Those involved in democratic politics – lobbyists, rights groups, the politicians themselves – depend on effective public relations. The best among them are open to new communications ideas and technology. Margaret Thatcher has recorded a moment of discovery which was of no small importance to her public image. It followed a speech by President Reagan in 1982, apparently delivered from memory:

> He replied, 'I read the whole speech from those two perspex screens' – referring to what we had taken to be some security device. 'Don't you know it? It's a British invention.' And so it was that I made my first acquaintance with Autocue.[14]

Because of alert politicians, the possibilities of public relations have expanded, and filtered into pressure groups and corporations. The more people you need to talk with, the more you must organize what you say. The truth of this guiding principle became apparent in the rough-and-tumble world of eighteenth-century England, as we have seen with Swift. It is often said of William Pitt the elder that he was the first British Prime Minister given by the people to the King. That popular legend is partly based on Pitt's sense of public relations during his rise to power in the 1750s. He was the first modern politician to comprehend that the classic combination of message, audience identification and delivery could be used to contact a large public, over the heads of the élite political class accustomed to traditional intrigue among themselves. Pitt's flash of insight made a sizeable impact on politics. One contemporary noted his communications abilities, which are worthy of any modern, trained, politician: 'He has a peculiar clearness and facility of expression; and has an eye as significant as his words. He is not always a fair or conclusive reasoner, but commands the passions with sovereign authority; and to inflame or captivate a popular assembly is a consummate orator.'[15]

Unlike the great landowners and their clients who traditionally held political power, Pitt was not rich, and he did not control any constituencies. He needed to identify larger and less exclusive audiences. In 1746 he was given his first official post, Paymaster-General. It was normal for anyone in that position to exploit it by skimming off the interest on the official budget, and to pocket bribes from foreign countries interested in British financial support. Pitt publicly announced that he would only accept his official salary, and no more. Popular cynicism at the corrupt habits of politicians was as great then as it is today, and so the effect of Pitt's announcement was immediate. 'A born actor, by this gesture he caught the eye of the people, and held it as no statesman had held it before him,' admired Winston Churchill.[16] Another, more matter-of-fact writer has agreed: 'Pitt's action in this respect was a major factor in the revival of a reputation for disinterested patriotism that had been shattered when he joined the Government.'[17] What is interesting about it is Pitt's method of unlocking the power of public opinion. This is a modern, sophisticated political public-relations tactic. With this action, Pitt sent out a message about himself that was more effective than a party political commercial. By realizing the value of a popular – as opposed to an élite – public image, Pitt helped father the clutter of current political communications: the autocue, the photo opportunities and demonstrations, the televised interviews. But Pitt also showed that he was quite sure about exactly which audience he needed to reach: he was not merely appealing to an indefinable and romantic wedge called 'the people'. His message was targeted. It went to the new, rising middle classes, the city financiers and traders whose money enriched Britain far beyond the means of her rivals. Their backing eventually secured his elevation to Prime Minister. The King and many traditional politicians opposed him, but Pitt by-passed them in favour of another, ultimately more influential, audience. He retained their support until 1766, when he finally accepted an earldom and a regular pension. This drastic reversal of the public image he had carefully cultivated over twenty years helped destroy his popularity, and eventually his power. 'Pitt's acceptance of a peerage was widely criticised.' A pamphlet: 'A Letter of Will Chat-em of Turn-about-Hall,' attacked the appointment. 'Lord Chat-em is now the object of universal detestation.'[18] Another complained: 'He was the only person of his time, who with specious pretences and harangues, could persuade the people their service only was the intended fruit of his labours,' until he accepted a peerage and sank 'into general discharge and contempt'.[19]

Pitt was a far-sighted communicator, and at the same time a victim of public relations. He had successfully 'marked well her grace' – anticipating the benefits to be gained from communicating a popular 'image' over the one he presented to colleagues (which was described at the time as 'imperious, violent and implacable'). But Pitt remained oblivious to communication's perils. While he depended upon public recognition of his selflessness and patriotism, he did not fully comprehend the independent power of public relations, or the extent of his reliance on the shining public image he had established among merchants and financiers, and in the political pamphlets that circulated in large numbers. When his public relations image was shattered, he was broken too. It has been remarked of that period: 'The cultivation of popularity now needed one who could break out of the cautious and condescending attitude to "the people" characteristic of most eighteenth century politicians into a more equal, direct and confident relationship.'[20] The principle has been respected since Pitt's time by politicians, governments and political parties.

PUBLIC RELATIONS: THE MASTER

Pitt discovered that communications can control as well as serve those pursuing power. Its mastery over influential people and organizations takes two forms; each morally questionable and hard to see in advance. First, publicity can act almost as a drug, intoxicating powerful people to abuse their position to achieve the public relations they personally desire. We have observed Montgomery's instinct for the sort of public relations required to build the morale and consequently the fighting effectiveness of his soldiers. His colleague, US General Mark Clark, led the Fifth Army slowly and painfully up Italy in the face of tough German resistance between 1943 and 1945. He also used public relations – but seemingly as much for his own benefit as his army's. A colleague and admirer of Clark's military talents conceded that 'his drive to reach the top sometimes causes him to seek personal publicity'.[21] Clark was well aware of the value of publicity. Earlier in the war he had made a daring submarine journey that, after a successful press conference, turned him into a national hero and helped him win command of the Fifth Army. 'Clark's concern with publicity', an admiring biographer has written, 'stemmed from his desire to make good in the normally fierce military rivalry.'[22]

The publicity battles between the Allied generals were occasionally as sharp as the real battles they fought against their common enemy. Clark's capture of Naples in October 1943 – the first major European city to be liberated – produced a request from the staff of Lord Alexander, Supreme Commander of the Allies in Italy. 'Alexander's public relations officer asked him to tell the press that British troops had entered Naples first.' Clark made the announcement, complains his biographer, 'even though American paratroopers and rangers had accompanied the British into the city'.[23] Nevertheless, Clark himself halted his army at the outskirts of Naples until he could come forward to enter the city personally accompanied by the press. To his surprise, the streets were empty. There were no cheering crowds. Naples resembled a ghost town. The reason was that while his troops awaited the arrival of their publicity-hungry leader, the Neapolitans were prostrate from appalling reprisals after their premature, bloody uprising against the retreating Germans. Clark nurtured his media relations all through the controversies of the Italian campaign. He was approachable, and knew how to attract journalists. One correspondent, invited to dinner by Clark, recorded: 'I found Clark very congenial, and straightforward too. He impressed me as a thoroughly honest man.'[24] He received fan mail from the United States: 'you seemed closer than the usual news story personality', one wrote. 'You were like someone we knew, whose daily doings we watched with friendly interest.'[25]

Notwithstanding his public-relations efforts, indeed partly because of them, Clark has been criticized; especially for his wish to win the credit for liberating Rome, the first European capital to be freed from the Nazis. Detractors say that he detached the main part of his army from the main assault against the Germans, enabling the enemy to escape and prolong the war in the peninsula.[26] In a famous incident, an aide from Clark's headquarters apparently told a field commander to wipe out the last pockets of resistance ahead of schedule so that Clark could free Rome as soon as possible. 'Why the hurry?' asked the commander, worried about the unnecessary risk to men's lives. 'France is going to be invaded from England,' Clark's aide answered. 'We've got to get this' – meaning the capture of Rome – 'in the newspapers before them.'[27] Clark entered Rome just in time: 'In the United States, many photographs in the press showed Clark at the Colosseum, driving through the streets of the city, at the Vatican.'[28] Alas, his efforts were indeed trumped by D-Day, which took place two days later. The half-written stories of Clark's media posse drifted to the ground. They knew that henceforth the Italian campaign was, in terms of news and publicity, a sideshow.

We have seen how the choice of the communications route shapes the way in which the message is sent, the way in which it is received by its audience, and the dependent position in which those using it can be placed. The second form of control occurs when those responsible for communications on behalf of the powerful realize that they possess the means of taking control for themselves. In Ming China the message-carrying medium happened to be human beings. Wanli, one of the longest reigning emperors of China's Ming Dynasty, became a recluse in the last years of the sixteenth-century. He remained inside his palace for 25 years, and restricted his communications to his palace servants, the eunuchs. They passed on his commands to the civil service outside the walls of the inner court. Eventually, the control they enjoyed over the messages and the means of communicating enlarged their own power and status. Their constant contact with the Emperor – the message-creating institution – allowed them to extend their job as imperial communicators. As well as passing on messages from the Emperor, they began travelling to the frontier to gather information for the Emperor. Officials used to regarding eunuchs as dirty and debased, were forced to live among them and watch as they accumulated great wealth. Finally, as two successive emperors stagnated in apathy, the eunuch–tyrant Wei Zhongxian took control of the government. The evolution of the eunuchs from obedient carriers of the Emperor's orders to arbiters of national policy happened very quickly. As the main means of imperial communications their rise from despised servants to advisers and ultimately controllers was virtually ordained.

Modern controllers of public relations are much more benign, but have the same capacity to create dependence among those they ostensibly serve. The main point of resemblance is that, as with Ming China, the innocent assumption of wider controls by the persons responsible for communications remains a threat to the work of the powerful. Modern democratic leaders seem as helpless as Chinese emperors, particularly in the United States of America. In former times, an American President was not held personally responsible for everything that occurred in the country. Petitioners were few, his physical features remained a mystery to most citizens. Even as late as the 1960s, the President's family members were not expected to submit themselves for public inspection. All this has changed thanks to a pact made between public-relations experts, ambitious politicians and the bloated, inward-looking Washington media corps. Counting up the daily 'appearances' made by modern political leaders in the manner of ancient monarchs or high priests, begs the question: when do they actually run the country? Communications has invaded the finances, corridors and offices of state, in order to deal with the increased public scrutiny of Government that it helped create. In the United States, teams exist to manage the President's press conferences, to write up masses of official opinions for public consumption, to arrange every detail of visits, tours and impromptu vacation appearances, to ensure re-election, to handle correspondence. There is a director responsible for the President's electronic mail.

The possibility of these well-paid communicators exploiting their role to bid for power is somewhat more remote than it was among the bitter eunuchs of sixteenth-century China. Less remote is the chance that, propelled by new communications technology creating new audiences and matters for debate, public relations' priorities – its sense of its own importance – will expand and force organizations to subvert worthier functions in order to serve its needs. We are so wired up to communications media, that how an argument reaches an audience seems as important in the process of persuasion as the actual argument itself. It is not a new consideration, but of late it has mushroomed. After a trip to Washington in the 1840s Dickens recorded that people rarely asked what a politician said, but for how long he spoke. 'These', he added, 'are but enlargements of a principle which prevails elsewhere.'[29] The principle continues to enlarge by exploiting new avenues of communication. As more and more organizations compete for our time, and our attention span has diminished, so has the detail of what politicians can tell us. In the nineteenth century and the early part of the twentieth century, politicians did speak for hours at a stretch. Curious people outside the capital wanted to make the most of their leaders because they rarely got to see them. Now we see them twenty times a day. They fight to divert our attention from other things: our holiday plans, baked beans, sports television, reading a novel. We can choose our entertainment – and so politicians adapt their messages to these circumstances, and try to reach millions of voters. Their messages get shorter and simpler, their political broadcasts contain distracting non-political embellishments: music and soft-focus images. Politicians hate seeing us walking out of the room or putting down our newspaper. They need to control the process as much as they can. 'In an age of advertisement great men can afford but few flashes of silence.'[30]

So preoccupied are leaders with the need to create or satisfy demands for public appearance and comment via various media that their communications advisers must intervene in policy. Differences between style and substance have grown indistinct, and dribble confusingly into each other. David Gergen directed the communications of four American Presidents from Nixon to Clinton. Few other people understand so well the metamorphosis of public relations from servant to master:

> Look, I plead guilty to having played the game and inventing some forms of the game that I thought eventually went beyond what was intended . . . It gave way over time to – and this is what I regret – a selling for the sake of selling. It had nothing to do with ideas. It had nothing to do with anything that was real. Eventually, it became the sizzle without the steak. There was nothing connected to it. It was all cellophane. It was all packaging.[31]

Where open political debate theoretically exists, there is a risk that public relations will flourish beyond the needs of free speech and smother debate in safe but meaningless platitudes. The monstrous role of public relations within the White House mirrors a similar if less lavish tendency at work elsewhere. Non-government organizations may have more modest communications requirements, yet there is still scope for public relations to expand beyond the limits of budgets and common sense. On occasion the existence of public relations can, ironically, damage the responsible organization. The Department of Education in Britain discovered this in summer 1994, when it was attacked for swelling its publicity budget from £100,000 to almost £9 million in fifteen years.[32]

It is necessary for public relations to work directly for power, and to possess power for itself. Without power, the communicators would be reduced to mouthpieces. It would be harder for powerful organizations to present convincing messages, or engage in dialogue with key audiences. Public relations is carving out a powerful position among the possessors of corporate and political authority. Nevertheless, 'it remains true', Aristotle commented in *Politics*, 'that the greatest injustices proceed from those who pursue excess, not from those who are driven by necessity'. The power accruing to the White House communications function prompts the older memory of Wei Zhongxian who, as we have seen, advanced his responsibility for communications to the point of supplanting the Emperor. Wei Zhongxian ended his career by consolidating his power with a communications programme of his own: giving adopted 'grandsons' the names of famous sages and emperors and erecting temples to himself. Different times lead to different abuses, but to abuses nevertheless.

NOTES

1 Brogan, Hugh. *History of the United States of America* (London: Longman, 1985) p 606.
2 Prendergast, Mark. *For God, Country, and Coca-Cola* (New York: Macmillan, 1993) pp 362–4.
3 Louis, J. C. and Yazijian, Harvey. *The Cola Wars* (New York: Everest House, 1980) pp 151–2.
4 Campbell, Joseph. *The Power of Myth*. With Bill Moyers (New York: Anchor 1991) p 38.
5 Prendergast, *For God, Country and Coca-Cola*, p 364.
6 Gardiner, Sir Alan. *Egypt of the Pharaohs* (Oxford: Oxford University Press, 1964) p 256.
7 Ibid.
8 Shelley, Percy Bysshe. 'Ozymandias' Published originally by Hunt in *The Examiner,* January 1818.
9 Lee, Ivy Ledbetter. *Publicity: Some of the things it is and is not*. (New York: Industries Publishing, 1925).
10 Selborne, David. *Death of the Dark Hero* (London: Cape, 1990) p 248.
11 Sandars, Nancy K. *The Sea Peoples*, rev. edn. (London: Thames & Hudson, 1985) p 31.
12 Gardiner, *Egypt of the Pharaohs*, p 256.
13 Webber, Alan M. 'The Statesman as CEO: An interview with Helmut Schmidt'. *Harvard Business Review*, July–August 1986, p 68.
14 Thatcher, Margaret. *The Downing Street Years* (New York: HarperCollins,) p 258.
15 Bigham, Hon. Clive. *The Prime Ministers of Britain* (London: Murray, 1922) p 80.
16 Churchill, Winston. *History of the English Speaking Peoples*, Volume 3. (London: Cassell, 1981 Fourth Edition) p 112.
17 Black, Jeremy. *Pitt the Elder* (Cambridge: Cambridge University Press, 1992) p 75.
18 Ibid., p 262.
19 Ibid., p 263.
20 Peters, Marie. *Pitt and Popularity* (Oxford: Oxford University Press, 1980) p 276.
21 Blumenson, Martin. *Mark Clark* (New York: Congdon & Weed, 1984) p 288.
22 Ibid., p 284.
23 Ibid., p 146.
24 Ibid., p 200.
25 Ibid., p 289.
26 For instance: 'Mark Clark making a beeline for Rome . . . was to have serious consequences for the subsequent prosecution of the war in Italy, providing the opportunity for the majority of Kesselring's forces to escape the Allied pincer and re-form on the line Florence–Rome.' Craster, Michael. 'Cunningham, Ritchie and Leese', in Keegan, John (ed.), *Churchill's Generals* (New York: Quill, 1991) p 216.
27 Blumenson, *Mark Clark*, p 216.
28 Ibid.
29 Dickens, Charles. *American Notes and Pictures from Italy* (Oxford: 1966 edn. First published 1864) p 122.
30 Lord Vansittart. *Lessons of My Life* (London: Hutchinson, *c.* 1944) p 88.
31 Kelly, Michael. 'David Gergen, Master of The Game'. *New York Times Magazine*, 31 October 1993, p 66.
32 'Tories 8.8m pound education "propaganda" attacked'. *Independent on Sunday*, 19 June 1994.

CHAPTER NINE

Lying and Evil in
Public Relations

Since truth is a matter of propositions, somebody must
make a proposition before a real fact becomes a true fact.[1]   John Bossy

And when they are in authority, are they also telling us lies? And when they do tell us lies, is it propaganda or public relations?

The philosopher Bertrand Russell reminded his readers:

> We all know what we mean by a 'good' man. The ideally good man does not drink or smoke, avoids bad language, converses in the presence of men only exactly as he would as if there were ladies present, attends church regularly, and holds the correct opinions on all subjects.[2]

Like Russell, most of us are prepared – possibly keen – to accept that human beings cannot be conventionally perfect. We are less prepared to be so understanding towards many large organizations, though they too are shaped by the flawed humans who toil for them. 'The earth is no paradise. Although this is not the fault of social institutions, people are wont to hold them responsible for it.'[3] Christ's lesson: 'He that is without sin among you, let him first cast a stone at her,' is the principle with which we rescue guilty people from outraged fellow sinners.[4] But it is very different for organizations. The larger of them, and their most prominent and well-paid representatives, are exposed to minute legal, political and media scrutiny. If they fail to meet our expectations, we criticize, demand punishment: resignations, perhaps incarceration. We attach the sorts of standards to impersonal organizations that we do not attach to ourselves as individuals. Like Dorian Gray's mirror, they reflect our own flaws and take the blows we cannot bring ourselves to inflict on the people around us. Perhaps our intensity of feeling stems from the fact that organizations affect all areas of our lives, for all of our lives. They exist to maintain, reward or punish us in various ways. Through them, whether church, charity or merchant bank, we try to build into society some of the virtue that gives our own lives standards. We can ignore certain individuals, but it is much harder to ignore organizations. We want them to behave with enough morality to justify their control over us.

That is why an organization's communications is so important: it is the outward sign of its inward character. Whenever their communicators fail to convince, we stop believing or accepting them. As we have already discovered, it can be a small step from failure to believe in an organization to a refusal to interact with it at all. Public relations is the herald of an organization's ethical position. Communicators are ideally the first to identify problems with an audience, and must handle the debate on their employer's behalf. Naturally, we sometimes confuse the message itself with the way they delivered it.

And that is one reason why people are sceptical about standards of behaviour in public relations. Public relations *has* undoubtedly transmitted lies and served evil. We must consider when, why and how. But we should proceed with caution. For one thing, criticism of bad public relations might deflect attention from the actual message itself, and so we lose sight of the real problem. Worse, our personal view of issues often stops us accepting the right of an organization to put forward ideas of its own. Then there is the constant emergence of new needs and technology to upset the equilibrium and open fresh, morally unregulated fields for communicators to enter. These are all problems of perception, and influence us when we make up our minds about the rightness of public relations. The problem of propaganda is closely related. It is a dirty word. It exploits public-relations techniques on behalf of perjury, compulsion and injustice. 'We can never say that public relations has nothing to do with propaganda,' one eminent commentator has observed, 'just as the propagandist can never say that he does not, from time to time, practise public relations.'[5] Public relations is fouled up with propaganda; it ranges over the ground between compulsion and free persuasion. That boundary, separating political and corporate propaganda from more gentle sorts of public relations, must be explored. It is where ethical judgement is rendered.

Given all these circumstances, public relations can hardly fail to earn itself a bad name. 'The great principle of the project was an evil of the first magnitude; it was to raise artificially the value of the stock, by exciting and keeping up a general infatuation and by promising dividends out of funds which would not be adequate to the purpose.'[6] This famous attack on the communications process rather than on the messages is supposed to have been made by Robert Walpole, who later became Britain's first Prime Minister. He was speaking in 1720, during the first boom in the London and Paris stock markets now remembered as the 'South Sea Bubble'. 'Exciting and keeping up a general infatuation' was his description of numerous promotions inciting people to sink their savings into anything that moved: companies claiming to make salt water fresh; wheels of perpetual motion; a machine-gun designed to discharge round bullets against Christians, and square ones against the Muslim Turks. 'It was enough for any man to take a room near 'Change alley, and advertise a "bubble" in the newspapers, for people to flock to him and beg him to take their money'.[7] Walpole's words are an indictment of the power of public relations. The Paris boom was ignited by the hype of a Scotsman, John Law. He used his skill to sell shares in the ill-fated Mississippi Company, responsible for developing French land in North America. 'Law's flair for publicity never flagged,' comments one student of the period. When a French officer brought back the daughter of an Indian chief, Law seized the publicity opportunity it offered. They were exhibited hunting in the Bois de Boulogne and dancing in the Italian theatre. 'The climax was reached when the chief's daughter agreed to be baptized in Notre Dame; and shortly afterwards announced that she would marry a French sergeant. Everyone was enchanted.'[8] Somehow, the publicity was mistaken for the message, which of course it was not. Law in Paris and numerous speculators in London were thought to have discovered the secret of limitless wealth, but since the bubbles were inflated by publicity alone they all burst. The falling shares ruined humble and wealthy investors alike (except Walpole, who was sensible enough to buy and sell at the right moment).

We are as blinded by the methods of public relations today, which is why people are suspicious when it is used by organizations with an image problem. On the other hand, manufacturers of pesticides and nuclear energy feel they have a perfect right to present their case. Lawyers are expected to represent the innocent as well as the guilty. If prisoners in the dock have that freedom, why not law-abiding corporations? Unfortunately for public relations, the belief that both sides of an argument are entitled to be heard is not a privilege we are always ready to extend beyond the courthouse. The upstart public relations is treated with suspicion; it lacks the splendid ornaments of legal procedure, which is sanctified by precedent. It is everywhere, hard to control. How, we wonder, could anybody bring themselves to communicate for a tobacco company, or a country with a dubious human-rights record, or a questionable religious cult? Some practitioners answer that public relations is neutral. It uses a set of freely available tools to present a particular message on a particular issue. Some argue that there is no such thing as a 'true' opinion, and that public debate is constantly shaped by our subjective interpretation of the facts and arguments presented to us. As long as a set of facts and arguments are honestly given and credited to their source, they are as permissible as any others. It is ironic that our fear of subversive agendas lurking behind innocent, 'objective' information has increased ever since corporations overcame their attachment to secrecy and used publicists to communicate their points of view openly .

Meanwhile, technology is also pushing public relations ahead of our understanding about what it might be doing to us. There are often too few ethical guidelines to distract the communicators from their attempts to capitalize on the exciting new tools. Margaret Thatcher's Department of Trade and Industry introduced semi-commercial techniques in the 1980s to advertise its job-training and business information services. Instead of a few pamphlets and the usual formal, dry ministerial announcement, bound by custom and parliamentary rulings, modern information techniques were employed, including a prominent Trade and Industry logo of a dynamically swooping arrow. Was the department advertising the service or itself? Was the campaign informing audiences about a new training product or was there an underlying hint of departmental propaganda on behalf of the Tories? 'The Government', remembered Thatcher's press chief Sir Bernard Ingham, 'was confronted with a situation in which the art of the publicist had moved so far and so fast that the political impartiality of Government publicity was in danger of being compromised.'[9] The fear of turning vivid ways of presenting information into party political commercials prompted an inquiry, which produced new guidelines that tried 'to balance technique with propriety'.[10] One of the most important sections warned:

> 'Image building', whether explicit or implied and whether of Government or Minister, is not acceptable. The test is whether a campaign, taken both as a whole or in part, can be justified as an effective response to a requirement to communicate with the public, or a particular section of it on an issue of importance.[11]

But public relations is everywhere, and hard to control. Who decides which issues deserve 'a requirement to communicate', and what, precisely, is 'an issue of importance'? Is not any expression of government policy, however it is communicated, an inevitable form of 'image-building'? Communication is essential to good government, which is after all formed by a party or coalition elected on the basis of an image and policies it feels are better than its rivals. It can hardly be expected to stop transmitting the messages that elected it, but crticism of its public relations as propaganda is inevitable since there is so much to communicate. When the Conservative Government prepared its Citizen's Charter programme, it launched an expensive publicity campaign to inform the people of their rights. It included a £3 million mail-out of the Parent's Charter on education to 20 million homes, 'despite the fact that Britain has fewer than five million homes with school-age children', noted the *Independent on Sunday*.[12] Critics said the whole brochure could have been confined to a single sheet of paper, and the money spent on easing class overcrowding and substandard buildings. Image-building like that brushes against the shoals of propaganda.

Is there a difference? At worst, propaganda is supposed to tell lies. At best, it squeezes public relations into compulsory and constricted forms. To a large extent, propaganda is in the eye of the beholder. If a Government health department decides to launch an anti-caffeine campaign, a critic from a beverage manufacturer might describe it as propaganda, that sends a one-sided view at the expense of taxpayers, many of whom drink coffee. A medical expert might defend the campaign as a worthy attempt to commun-icate important information on a health issue. Propaganda seems more obvious in repressive or unstable societies. In times of flux and social break-down movements seek active support or at least silent agreement from large numbers of people. The Protestant Reformation in the sixteenth century was a crucial moment for communications. Large quantities of pamphlets, car-toons, and posters were issued by interested groups or individuals. These approaches to educated and uneducated alike were for the most part pro-duced at random by talented enthusiasts; not by a State communications bureaux following a detailed and carefully targeted plan. One distinctive case of state communications from this time should be recorded. Sir Thomas Cromwell 'had subsidised plays which were performed in town squares and village greens throughout England in order to rub in King Henry VIII's case against the Papacy'.[13] When plans are laid to change the official religion of a nation, even the strongest ruler must make an attempt to persuade public opinion. Cromwell understood the need to send his master's messages past the powerful, and direct to the common people, who could be coaxed but not compelled to change their personal beliefs. The power of theatre to send a verbal or visual message is periodically rediscovered by governments, as well as playwrights, particularly in largely illiterate societies like sixteenth-century England. In the late 1980s, the Egyptian ministry of culture tried to ease tensions between Muslims and the minority Coptic Christians by spon-soring a series of popular plays.

From these lengthy quarrels between religious institutions, individuals, and rulers in sixteenth-century Europe, the word propaganda eventually entered the English language; arriving by the early eighteenth century and drawn from the term 'Congretatio de propaganda fide', or 'propagating the faith'. This was the full name of the 'Propaganda', a committee of Roman Catholics charged in 1622 with 'the dissemination of the Christian faith, through which men may be brought to the knowledge and adoration of the true God'.[14] By the mid-nineteenth century the word had given birth to 'pro-pagandism', 'propagandist', 'propagandize' and included the relentless promotion of doctrines or practices by any association. Napoleon was an early master of propaganda, declaring that 'if the press were not bridled, I would not remain three days in power'.[15] Art and literature were encouraged to present his subjects with the conflicting images of an all-conquering Emperor fighting the cause of revolutionary liberty. Napoleon, unlike pre-revolutionary monarchs, was not regarded as Divine or Divinely ordained. A revolution in thought and politics barred him from partaking of the religious aura that surrounded older dynasties. The maintenance and majesty of his rule depended on him alone, definitely unassisted by the Heavenly Host. He aspired to world conquest, and relied on an army recruited from the nation, embodying the national will to co-operate. The monarchs who opposed him with mercenaries and professional armies demanded less from their subjects; their rule was legitimized by custom and habit. Napoleon, though, had to motivate his subjects to support his conquests and to accept the daily sacrifices his plans required. He was well aware that propaganda was imperative to his domestic and international ambitions.

In constructing his propaganda, Napoleon formed a very modern notion of the importance of communications. 'Government is nothing unless supported by opinion,' he once remarked. Another, more worrying comment of his was: 'The truth is not half so important as what people think to be true.'[16] Napoleon took an intense interest in the press, and in the control of what would now be called key messages. His grip of propaganda rivals his grasp of the military arts. Both were central to his authority. Before the electronic age compressed time to bring us vast quantities of news and information about an event within moments of it happening, it was much easier for men like Napoleon to deliver 'what people think to be true'. On one notorious occasion in 1805, he received news of the British naval victory at Trafalgar off the Spanish coast, the greatest naval disaster in French history. It had taken 26 days to reach him. Trafalgar saved Britain from invasion and ensured her command of the sea for over a century. Napoleon's immediate reaction was censorship. 'Rarely', one historian believes, 'has there been such a total news blackout.'[17] The French press was shut up for another three weeks, at which time, redeemed by his own land victories at Ulm and Austerlitz, Napoleon's semi-official government newspaper announced that a great naval battle had taken place off Trafalgar. Nineteen British ships, it claimed, were sunk or burned (the actual figure was nil out of 27), as against minimal French and Spanish losses (the true figure was 23 out of 33). 'This report attests brilliantly to the worth of the French fleet,' the newspaper claimed, although that fleet no longer existed.

Napoleon also had a strong belief in the public-relations power of spectacles and festivals. A favourite ploy of his was to send captured enemy flags to a public body like the Senate, surrounded by pageantry. He flung himself deeply into the tiniest details of these events, knowing the value of their impact on domestic and international audiences. The basic idea is timeless, and has been employed in the twentieth-century by governments of all stripes, and the best-intentioned companies and other organizations. May Day for Communists, Mothers Day for mothers, Earth Day for environmentalists, No-smoking Day for non-smokers. Courteous smoking day for smokers. Prostate cancer awareness week. Year of the child. We are glutted with commemorations. The real task is for each event to convey its meaning in a way that will survive the short-lived festivities.

The chief difference between dangerous Napoleonic spectacle and good-hearted Earth Day is, curiously, the presence or otherwise of silence. Public relations becomes propaganda when it speaks into a void created by censorship or the total restriction of free speech. 'What is truly vicious is not propaganda, but a monopoly of it,' the *New York Times* averred in 1937.[18] Public relations developed from the need to compete in the presentation of messages to audiences. Its techniques degenerate into propaganda whenever speech is curtailed, when it tries to present subjective points of view as truths, and when the audiences are denied or discouraged from seeking alternative information. It is undeniably simpler for public relations to 'propagate the faith', if the object of that faith is an earthly leader with no tolerance for rivals. The Italian Dictator Mussolini, a former newspaper editor who took power in 1922, was obsessed with the importance of the press, and of controlling the news and particularly his own image. He frequently commented that Italy was 'a land of theatre and its leaders must orchestrate their public contacts'.[19] He flattered journalists by telling them, just as Napoleon told his humblest troops, that they perhaps carried Field-Marshals batons in their knapsacks. Half of his ruling Fascist Grand Council were journalists. Dozens were made senior diplomats, and members of parliament. *Il Duce* boasted he read hundreds of newspapers every day – he once claimed the figure was 350 – getting to know the styles of individual journalists.[20] This is good going for a junior public-relations account executive, but it should not be the main priority for the leader of a country. Mussolini considered his press office so important that its manager sometimes attended cabinet meetings, and met with his leader several times a day. Mussolini himself would telephone newspapers with orders about content and even front-page layout. There is great value in giving public relations a role in shaping an organization's fundamental policies, but it is dangerous to make public relations into the sole policy. Mussolini's public-relations mistake was to send lies into a vacuum, and to invest such energy in the process that he came to believe them himself and would not give serious attention to more substantial wartime matters such as supporting his troops and the poor state of Italy's industry. In the end, Fascism was propped up by little more than publicity and random intimidation.

Shortly before Goebbels, Stalin, Mussolini, Mao and others of their kidney grasped the potential of propaganda and used modern technology to control or silence communications they disliked, the early inter-war pioneers of public relations were hoping to make propaganda a justifiable branch of their work, a benign force for promoting understanding between nations in difficult times. 'Who was it said you cannot hate a man you really know?' asked Ivy Lee in 1934 – one year after Hitler had taken power in Germany. Lee proposed that 'legitimate international propaganda' had a role to play, despite the fact that it was so 'polluted, poisoned and prostituted that it is difficult to think of it in its strictly derivative sense'.[21] Part of the problem, he argued, was that the process was expressed through the convoluted jargon of diplomatists and lawyers.

Lee believed that useful propaganda, which he interpreted as the open communication of a nation's opinion, did not need to tell lies. Rameses, for instance, had upheld a connected principle of Lee's: that 'honest' propaganda is those opinions which carry the 'signature' of its source. Since Abu Simbel has Rameses' name and image all over it, it amply fulfils Lee's criteria. Is that honesty enough to endorse Rameses' propaganda? Lee also believed that honest propaganda should contain no false statements. By the standards of his time, Rameses' messages were truthful. He doubtless believed himself divine, in common with all the other Pharaohs. But to see Rameses depicted on the wall of his temple coolly stalking over the corpses of Hittite warriors forces one to question whether openness is a morally sufficient definition. Public relations, with its power to communicate messages to millions of people, has a deeper responsibility. From this perspective, it is a short step from Abu Simbel to the efforts of certain twentieth-century communicators to raise leaders and beliefs far above the rest and perpetrate measureless cruelty in the process.

The gathering of people in cities, offices and factories has made it essential, and in time simple, for leaders to reach this mass with messages. Without the organized commitment or consent of the urban world, policies cannot be understood or followed. This was an unprecedented circumstance at the turn of the twentieth century. 'It is strange to remember,' noted Harold Macmillan, a perceptive political communicator and witness to our century, 'that at that time and indeed until the early twenties, a Government had no method of communication with the public except through the Press.'[22] When the First World War broke out in 1914, communications technology had still not caught up with the unprecedented political requirement to mobilize the industrial nations for conflict. Other than speeches and posters 'there was nothing except the communiqués, which were uninformative, to guide the public mind'.[23] Macmillan himself went on to exploit television technology to great effect in his prime ministerial career. Today, the consequences of hearing from our representatives solely through newspapers and communiqués would be profound. A welcome peace to some, maybe, but fewer avenues for communications would raise daunting obstacles to open dialogue and prevent mass participation in debating national decisions.

In the late nineteenth-century, the emerging power of city societies led some to investigate 'the crowd': the phenomenon of strangers regularly gathered together en masse to protest, to demonstrate, to celebrate. Philosophers, authors and psychologists studied the best ways in which ambitious persons and institutions could harness its energy. Hitler unfortunately hit upon the direct route: through communications. He believed the mass meeting was the answer. The newspaper was 'so chopped up and so divided in its effect that looking at it once cannot be expected to have any influence on the reader'.[24] The leaflet 'will provide only a slight impetus'; it 'can only suggest or point to something'.[25] Hitler was an indifferent writer, and in any case interested in securing obedience from his listeners, not conversations with them. He preferred to exploit the individual 'from his little workshop or his big factory, in which he feels very small', through the agency of the rally, at which:

> The will, the longing, and also the power of thousands are accumulated in every individual. The man who enters such a meeting doubting and wavering leaves it inwardly reinforced: he has become a link in the community.[26]

The perils of knowing how to communicate with lonely urban humanity are obvious. The numerous abuses of the past sixty years have not slaked society's tremendous thirst for knowledge and for a place on the communications highways. Freely exchanged, communication can help people to make mature judgements on matters that interest them. It can allow us to accept or reject movements, rather than follow blindly. No modern organization or state can hope to survive without the co-operation of millions of informed individuals; even the harshest, most dictatorial companies or countries ultimately depend on the people they are mistreating. Lee sincerely hoped that international propaganda, the simple, clear presentation of points of view, would spread understanding between peoples and end the prospect of war. He believed that because there is good and bad in all of us, right is therefore a question of perception and greater understanding was all that was needed to settle disputes. This was a miscalculation, as Lee himself found when he chose to counsel Nazi Germany on its US communications via a contract with the German Dye Trust.[27] It ruined his career. Forms of rightness must remain absolute, and when the Second World War broke out a few years after Lee's downfall, many peoples experienced the absolute evil men can do. 'The truth about atrocities is far worse than that they are lied about and made into propaganda,'[28] wrote Orwell. 'The truth is that it happens.' Several times this century, the garish mask of protective propaganda has been ripped aside by those it failed to capture or convince, revealing to them slave states and ancient habits of tyranny equipped and organized with the torments of science.

But not everything Lee argued about propaganda has become redundant. He was optimistic about the ability of radio, the newspaper advertisement and the motion picture to present arguments and positions, rather than to issue threats and hatred. He hoped that technology would be used as a harmonious instrument in the concert of nations. The capitalist world is eagerly exploiting these tools for the honest presentation of products and points of view; for the promotion of dialogue, rather than aggression. The liberal societies of the west are wary of the power of communications tools and use greater prudence and wisdom when sending their messages. Abuse of course is still possible, but it is easier to contain it. Most organizations today are in the virtuous position of wishing acceptance for their own messages, but not at the cost of censoring others. For every organization attempting to send out its message, another is communicating an alternative. The place where they meet is our security, the most reliable guarantee of a neutral core, a 'common basis of agreement.' Public relations is at the service of those who have something to say – it is their responsibility to preserve for others the same opportunity. Without free speech, public relations dwindles into propaganda. It loses its creative impulse, and drifts away from the audiences who must hear it in any case because they are denied alternative communications by order of the state. It becomes harder to maintain conviction in a propaganda message. It seizes up since there is no need to compete for the tastes and preferences of its audiences. It eventually loses touch completely, and in doing so undermines its messages by failing to present them in a way audiences find credible. In the end, the response to pure propaganda is cynical, indifferent or angry; it destroys itself by failing to arouse the energy and commitment required to keep autocracies functioning.

The Romanian communist dictator Nicolae Ceausescu showed no imagination in his communications. He filled the press and national television with the same messages about himself year after year, refusing to adapt his propaganda to new circumstances, including economic collapse, until Romanians stopped listening, and eventually ceased to obey. The end of the *epocha Ceausescu* was triggered by one stale communications event too many. A 'Working People's Meeting' of eighty thousand disbelieving, tired and hungry Romanians was herded together by the leader's minions on 21 December 1989. They were expected to hold the usual banners, chant the usual slogans, and acclaim their ruler's address. But they were no longer prepared to be intimidated. The ensuing collapse was accelerated by yet another form of communications. The official broadcast of that last rally managed to relay clearly heard shouts of protests before shocked censors pulled the plug. Too late: after years of iron control, a vigorous, believable and very different message had escaped into the ether. According to one commentator:

> Television viewers and radio listeners scattered to share the news with neighbours who had missed the broadcast or to discuss the significance of the interruption. Until a few minutes before hardly any of these people would have dared to discuss a political event more or less openly with people they hardly knew. Now everyone knew that it was the beginning of the end.[29]

One of the most important events in the ensuing uprising was the early capture of the state-controlled television station. From there a dramatic and uncensored message of change went to watching Romanians and an astonished world. The television station was cleverly exploited by the revolutionaries. Suspicions even exist that many of the key moments of the revolution were faked, staged exclusively for the media by the former communists who eventually took power in Romania.[30] This necessity for public manipulation is a recent development. In past times, coups and countries were the preserve of the privileged few, and the concentration of weaponry and ideals made active support from the majority less urgent. When William II of England was killed in 1100, his younger brother Henry rode straight for the royal treasury to gain possession of it ahead of the rest of his family. Modern usurpers must persuade the rest of us to co-operate, and so they ride for the networks. Jean du Plessis, a self-styled 'Boer Commando', helps guard Radio Pretoria, a mouthpiece for extreme white South African conservatives. The radio station is fortified by guns and sandbags. Du Plessis says he is prepared to die defending Radio Pretoria; he believes that unyielding traditionalists can 'express ourselves, and our thoughts, with this radio station'.[31] If people like du Plessis are capable of sacrificing themselves for communications, it is hardly surprising that others try to control or organize it in order to meet their needs.

Propaganda dresses up instruction as information or opinion. It is compulsory, an indication of the official line that all must follow, at least in public. Content fails to respect style, which usually whithers on the vine. Here are a series of 'key messages' issued by North Korea's Central News Agency for domestic and foreign consumption.

On the North Korean economy:

A new great progress has been made in all fields of Socialist construction, though the targets of the total scope of industrial output and some major indices including electric power, steel and chemical fiber envisaged in the third seven-year plan failed to be attained due to international events and the acute situation created in Korea . . .

No politico-ideological offensive, economic blockade and military threat on the part of the imperialists and reactionaries can ever frighten the Korean people and no force on earth can block them from advancing under the leadership of the party.

9 December 1993

On the 52nd birthday of current dictator Kim Jong Il:

An endless stream of people are visiting the old home at Mount Paektu secret camp, the time-honored holy place of revolution where

> Comrade Kim Jong Il was born . . . With his rare leadership ability the Dear Leader has brilliantly carried out the many difficult and complex tasks in accomplishing the socialist cause of our times, performing immortal feats for the times and the revolution.
>
> 16 February 1994[32]

Style is irrelevant if the outcome is pre-ordained. The propagandist writes to a pre-set formula, and probably does not care whether North Koreans believe the message or not. The ability to keep propaganda alive by displays of imagination is thankfully rare in totalitarian regimes, because the free expression that acts as an incentive for creative communications is suppressed. Any imagination that remains is expressed by dwindling bands of true believers, who can manage instructive surprises. The early enthusiasts for the 1918 Russian Revolution sent messages through all sorts of media: architecture, art, music and film. Enthusiastic Soviet propagandists also took over the Imperial porcelain factory and produced attractive plates intended to bring news of the Communist era to the dinner tables of Soviet citizens. The wrecked economy soon made the tableware too expensive for locals. Much of it was exported, perhaps the only example of crockery as international communications. Preaching plates were traditional in Czarist Russia, where they bore Biblical quotations. What makes the communist porcelain different, an exercise in controlled communications, is the design's subservience to political requirements; the carefully prepared messages made for them to carry; and the fact that they were made for a human not divine force, interested in teaching the code of a completely new form of society. 'He who does not work, does not eat', one plate warns in a jazzy typescript, bearing pictures of a food ration card and Lenin's head. This particular message was carried on propaganda posters and even made it into the Soviet constitution. 'Land to the Workers', demands another plate, in strong red set in rich green around factories and stooks of wheat. In the end, the Soviet regime's communications went the way of all totalitarian states, settling into formulate messages, set ways of communicating and morally undermining itself in the process. 'Porcelain public relations' lasted just ten years.[33]

A fiendish and rare exception to the rule that imaginative public relations dies once it becomes propaganda is the career of Joseph Goebbels, Hitler's Minister for Propaganda. Goebbels, unlike his equivalents in other totalitarian regimes, kept German acceptance of Nazi rule more or less intact until its final destruction in 1945. He did this by ensuring that his means of communicating, and more importantly, his messages, responded to changes in circumstances. He never completely denied that new conditions required new approaches, and he always wrapped enough of the truth up in his carefully concocted messages to hold the active attention and support of large numbers of Germans. Goebbels combined a surprisingly wide view of communications with great ability to organize. He saw that the press was only one channel for Nazi propaganda, and that all forms of public expression had a public-relations value. He quickly took command of most of them, from newspapers to theatre and fine art. All were isolated into compulsory 'Chambers' led by Nazis and placed at the service of the regime. Worse, Goebbels studiously avoided the crude self-serving propaganda of other dictatorships. He preserved elements of persuasion in his messages to convey the impression of free choice and open dialogue when in fact none existed. One of Goebbels' senior executives told the Allies: 'Had we actually lied in a thousand little ways, it would have been far easier for the enemy to deal with us effectively.' Goebbels 'would blow up small events, embellish crimes that had been perpetrated'.[34] Unlike Hitler, he had the sense to avoid hate and racial dogma in his propaganda. Goebbels dressed his messages in subtle guises. He held joyous festivals and rallies to maintain the momentum of Hitler's revolution. Rather than blatantly deny the German disaster at Stalingrad, he presented it as a heroic sacrifice and as the inspiration for his call for a national commitment to total war. An 'Action Jollity' campaign kept spirits up with organized humour when the war took a conclusive turn for the worse. As a contemporary perceived, too many people remained 'completely blind to the way they are being led, the way they are passing on ideas and phrases which have been put into their minds and mouths by a subtle master of revolutionary technique. In their weakness they imagine that the ideas are their own.'[35] Goebbels performed the nearly-impossible trick of successfully adjusting a totalitarian message to cope with a deteriorating situation and a bloodstained tyranny.

Even in contemporary and freer societies, public relations can serve compulsion. When it does, it becomes more insidious than totalitarian propaganda since it is harder to identify, and disguises compulsion as persuasion. Many corporations run education programmes with schools. Are they disinterested attempts to help pupils, or do they introduce uncontradicted sets of ideas about corporate practices to impressionable people? An American food and beverage company sponsored a 'solid waste school' to stress its own environmental responsibility, but also to educate future consumers about solid waste. A first class of 30 teachers of twelve- to fourteen-year-olds attended the month-long summer school, which included lectures and field trips on the creation and disposal of solid waste. A curriculum was developed for teaching to pupils, and the summer-school 'students' were trained to apply it. Finally, the curriculum was distributed to almost sixty thousand junior high schools, in the hope that it would be adopted. Should that audience find it hard to access other views, the corporation's view ceases to be a fair exercise of opinion to students, and becomes one-sided propaganda hidden behind the mechanism of free expression.

One person's truth will always be disreputable 'public relations' to another.

The question of compulsion in such cases is harder to resolve. If a sponsoring organization prepared an apparently balanced education package full of facts and alternative arguments about waste, can the user be absolutely certain that the sponsor's own position has not been given an unfair, hidden, advantage? An architect in ancient Egypt dutifully carved his ruler's name in majesty on the side of his tomb. He also inscribed his own name, set to one side. But he had chosen soft stone for Pharaoh, and durable rock for himself. Gradually, the theoretically immortal Pharaoh's name faded from his own tomb, leaving only the crafty architect's name intact, preserved and known to remote posterity. If, on the other hand, an educational programme is prepared that tries to put across scientific findings on solid waste, does it really matter which corporation or environmental group sponsored it? Does every point of view on a problem always need to be heard, regardless of what it actually says? Is every green crticism on corporations and their contribution to the world's mounting mountain of waste automatically better, more accurate and honest – especially when presented as an objective 'truth' by a convinced and respected person, such as a teacher?

Public relations can feel compulsory to a democratically minded audience when it is directed by an inappropriate organizing authority, and when it seals off alternative views by pursuing only one line of argument. The United Way's annual campaigns are a common feature of North American business life. This enormous charity co-ordinates excellent fund-raising drives for a multitude of good causes. Naturally, it targets businesses. Across the continent, many executives give a great deal of time to the fund-raising effort, to thinking of interesting ways to encourage donations from their colleagues. Their efforts consume valuable working hours, stationery, and office space for events or collection points. Many employers are generous with their facilities. Huge sums are raised over two to three weeks and sent to United Way, which distributes them among several hundred worthy causes across the continent. This is a tale of positive public relations, with thousands of bright, busy people engaged in a good cause. That, certainly, is the perspective of United Way. They welcome every penny, and are quick to congratulate and maintain good relations with the most generous givers. Many corporations are proud of their record, and use the event to advertise their contributions and their social conscience. Effective communications is central to good fund-raising, and, to encourage corporate America, United Way helps with advice and holds an annual communications contest with prizes for the biggest commercial contributors.

Some of the more enthusiastic companies take the fund-raising process a step further. Since it takes time and costs money, it seems fair to build the process into the corporation's business goals. Take the recent case of a small engineering consultancy. It employed less than 300 people, but it also had a reputation to maintain as one of United Way's biggest contributors. As an exercise in employee public relations, the campaign was undeniably small-scale, but impressive. The audience was obvious, but staff departures left a potential shortfall that threatened the company's fund-raising target. A number of new partners had been appointed. 'Most had just joined the firm and were not familiar with our commitment to United Way. Gaining their support would be key to the campaign's success,' wrote a campaign co-ordinator. 'We set an aggressive goal of $96,000 (9.4 per cent above [last year's] pledge).' The campaign team was advised that 'an aggressive dollar goal wasn't enough'; it had to 'have fun' too: 'We wouldn't pressure,' they decided, 'but we would ask for a sale.' They wisely used the programme to meet other company priorities: the chance for new people to get to know each other, and to demonstrate appreciation for all contributions.

The friendly approach was officially inaugurated with a campaign breakfast and no speeches, since 'attendance at the formal campaign kick-off had been falling for the last few years'. A personal letter to employees urging their participation was sent by the Chairman; computer software was used to plan and manage the work schedule. As with any big public-relations campaign, the team prepared a logo and theme: 'working together as a community, for our community', which appeared on all written material. A fund-raising team was picked, asked to sign an 'I'm committed' poster, handed team pins to wear for the campaign, and packets for each employee which included the all-important pledge card with the employee's name already filled in, a list of supported agencies and a United Way campaign leaflet. The company Chairman sent letters to all partners stressing the need for their commitment; a 'thermometer poster' was provided to keep employees up to date with progress. Prize draws were arranged for all contributors, with some undeniably attractive prizes, though perhaps not exactly in the spirit of this particular cause – winning executives looked forward to receiving two airline tickets and two nights in a hotel anywhere in the US, tea for six at a local hotel, five days' vacation. Different levels of 'giving' were established on the United Way guidelines of 'fair share', and 'fair share plus'. At the close of the campaign, employees discovered that they were 'among the most generous' in the area. The number of contributors increased by several per cent: 'we converted several long-time holdouts, with two of them jumping right into the fair share category', announced the campaign organizer to her team. Over $90,000 was raised. 'When you break open your cookie, remember the good fortune your contribution is bringing to others,' the team wrote to all contributors, imaginatively enclosing a fortune cookie with a note of thanks.

'Committed team member', read the badges handed out to the money-raisers, and there is no doubting the commitment, imagination and organization that lay behind the initiative. When the Chairman 'invites' you to a launch breakfast, you might just decide to go along. 'Be enthusiastic', urges an overhead slide in the presentation to fund-raisers. Well, better be enthusiastic. 'No pressure', pledges another nicely drawn slide. That is company tradition. Fund-raisers must 'promote good feelings'. Pledge cards cannot simply be sent. They must be accompanied by a personal visit in which you should: 'Have fun, smile and show your appreciation for their support!' If a personal visit from a fund-raiser, accompanied by a personal message from the company Chairman were not enough to rub in the 'voluntary' nature of the effort, fund-raisers were informed that nobody was allowed not to join in, even if they chose not to contribute. 'It is important to remind employees to return their card, even if they do not wish to participate in the program. If we have the card, then they won't be contacted again.' United Way has some good advice to those supporting these corporate-led efforts. 'Try to determine whether the contributor's objection is a reason or an excuse.' 'Turn any excuse into a positive reason for giving.' In fact, United Way is pretty adept at prising money from the reluctant. 'If your colleague is unable or unwilling to contribute at the Fair Share level, ask for a Trendsetter pledge.'[36]

A pedestrian, undeniably thorough, fund-raising effort had ended successfully and on the face of it had effectively employed several simple public-relations tools: a target audience, a clear objective, a series of key messages, creation of a vivid campaign identity by good design and motivation of team members, a range of tactics to drive those messages home. Personal notes and visits, a prize draw, nicely designed written materials, constant updates and monitoring of the programme. What was the clue to its success? Was it the efforts of the 'committed team members', or simply a near-unanimous outburst of spontaneous generosity? If this were all, it would scarcely be worth recounting. But of course the visible public relations tools are secondary to the murkier public relations that had taken place before the campaign began. The campaign merely decided the final extent of a victory that another, and much more questionable, form of communications had already won. Is there a sense here of compulsion? Has the Good Cause meshed itself too closely into winning a 'sale', and into the corporate culture as a whole? When your payroll is prepared to deduct for United Way on your behalf, you know how deeply the company leaders have integrated fund-raising; when you are personally contacted by the Chairman, then visited by 'fund-raisers', told to 'have fun' and reminded of the company commitment to giving, is it surprising if some find it prudent to tick 'yes' on their pledge card? If the company decides to organize and devote resources to the fund-raising, is the team motivated by a genuine interest in the plight of the less fortunate, or by a more pressing need to perform to the best of their ability? Should a donation be treated as a sale? Does the internal public-relations fund-raising become a commercial rather than a charitable exercise, with 'aggressive' rather than 'suggested' goals?

'As an officer and leader of the firm,' wrote the Chairman, 'I hope you will join me as a leader in this important campaign.' Important for what reason? Because it helps good causes, or because the covert, perhaps unintentional, messages sent out in the campaign's public relations makes it prudent not to refuse? The Chairman is more than ready to offer counsel: 'I hope you will consider a minimum of $150 a month. Last year's average officer contribution was $1600.' Pressure or advice? The final memo sent to recalcitrants opened:

> We are at the end of our annual United Way campaign period and would like to wrap up our record keeping activities.
>
> To date we have not received your pledge card.

It continued:

> If you have decided not to participate, we still need you to return a card for our records. Please just write 'No' on the pledge card, sign it and return it to me.

Whatever the targets of this public-relations campaign, it certainly capitalized on an odd mix of feelings: natural generosity, and maybe concern at being excluded from what on occasion sounds more like a matter of corporate policy than one of personal conscience. Giving should be a human, not a corporate matter. Charity and generosity should not be shut out of the workplace, but neither should they be formally integrated into a company's official communications. In those conditions public relations ceases to inform and adopts a sterner role.

WHATEVER THE PARTY DECIDES, WE WILL DO, exhorts a poster in North Korea.[37] The difference between doing what the party decides and doing what the company decides can be a fine one. Public relations does itself a disservice when it is harnessed to semi-compulsory messages, when it masks commands as 'fun', or recoils from clarifying whether a message is a command or not. The corporatization of western life is already pretty thoroughly advanced: must corporations now act as semi-compulsory guides in matters of personal conscience? When the charities sold their worthy causes to the boardrooms of North America, they inevitably made sympathetic companies see charity as a business issue. There is an ethical case for reviewing the charitable message to business leaders, and for refining an alternative. When a hierarchical corporation takes over a moral matter, and uses its official public relations to talk about it, well-intentioned exhortations decay into threats.

NOTES

1 Bossy, John. *Giordano Bruno and the Embassy Affair* (London: Vintage, 1991) p 2.

2 Russell, Bertrand. 'The harm that good men do', *Sceptical Essays*. (London: Routledge, 1991. First published in 1928) p 85.

3 Von Mises, L. *Liberalism in the Classical Tradition* (New York: Foundation for Economic Education, 1985. 3rd edition) p 63.

4 St John 8:7.

5 van der Meiden, A. Cited in Travers-Healy, Tim. 'Public relations and propaganda – Values compared'. *IPRA Gold Paper*, No 6, April 1988, p 11.

6 Cowles, Virginia. *The Great Swindle: The Story of the South Sea Bubble* (London: Collins, 1960) pp 42–3.

7 Ibid., p 62.

8 Ibid., p 96.

9 Ingham, Bernard. *Kill the Messenger* (London: Fontana, 1991) p 374.

10 Ibid.

11 Ibid., p 375.

12 *Independent on Sunday*, 19 June 1994.

13 Calvocoressi, P. and Wint, G. *Total War* (London: Allen Lane, 1972) p 505.

14 Cited in Neill, Steven. *A History of Christian Missions* (London: Penguin, 1986. 2nd edition) p 152.

15 Bowle, John. *Napoleon* (London: Weidenfeld & Nicolson, 1973) p 86.

16 Holtman, Robert B. *Napoleonic Propaganda* (Baton Rouge: Louisiana State University Press, 1950) p v.

17 Schom, Alan. *Trafalgar: Countdown to Battle, 1803–1805* (London: Penguin, 1992) p 362.

18 *New York Times*, 1 September 1937.

19 Mack Smith, Denis. *Mussolini* (London: Granada, 1983) p 145.

20 Ibid., p 79.

21 Lee, Ivy L. 'The problem of international propaganda. A new technique necessary in developing understanding between nations. An address by Ivy Lee delivered before a private group of persons concerned with international affairs, in London, July 3, 1934'. *Occasional Papers*. No. 3 (USA) p 9.

22 Macmillan, Harold. *Winds of Change* (London: Macmillan, 1966) p 60.

23 Ibid.

24 Hitler, Adolf. *Mein Kampf* (Boston: Houghton Mifflin, 1971. First published 1925) p 477.

25 Ibid., p 478.

26 Ibid., p 479.

27 Hainsworth, Brad E. 'Ivy Lee and the German Dye Trust'. *Public Relations Review*, XIII, no. 1 (Spring 1987) pp 35–44.

28 Orwell, George. *Homage to Catalonia* (London: Penguin, 1980) p 229

29 Almond, Mark. *The Rise and Fall of Nicolae and Elena Ceauescu* (London: Chapmans, 1992) p 6.

30 A returning dissident wrote: 'In truth, there were two revolutions: a real revolution that was not televised and that continues, particularly in Timisoara, and a studio revolution that fooled the entire world.' He later continued: 'Today I stand abashed by my naivete. Much of that Romanian "spontaneity" was as slick and scripted as a Hollywood movie. If I were in charge of the Emmys, I'd give one to the Romanian

directors of December 1989.' Codrescu, Andrei. *The Hole in the Flag* (New York: Morrow, 1991) pp 203–6.

31 'Good morning democracy: the media response to change in South Africa'. BBC2. 27 April 1994, 11.15pm–12.00.

32 'Mouthpiece of the "Great Leader": Bombast, Bile and Bowling News'. *The New York Times*, Sunday, 20 February 1994, Section 4, p 7.

33 From the collection of Craig and Kay Tuber of Chicago, USA.

34 Reimann, Viktor. *Joseph Goebbels: the Man who Created Hitler* (London: Sphere, 1979) p 241.

35 Rauschning, cited in Lord Vansittart, *Lesson of My Life* (London: Hutchinson, *c.* 1944) p 41.

36 'Six steps to a successful solicitation'. United Way pocket guide.

37 'Inside a new nuclear nemesis'. *Newsweek*, 21 February 1994, pp 28–9.

CHAPTER TEN

Truth and Purity and the Threat of the Perfect Message

So if there's so much publicity, why do we still know so
little about what's going on? The first answer is obvious:
that's not what publicity is for. It doesn't produce daylight
but arc-lights which show up the good bits and leave the
rest still darker.[1]
Anthony Sampson

Public relations is not always treated with respect. Justifiably so: it can be the smooth protective shield hiding numerous corporate misdemeanours. Many intelligent and well-informed people feel it distorts facts with trivia and staged distractions. In reply, its defenders might argue that the 'truth' of an issue grows less absolute in proportion to the number of available messages. They might add that one person's truth is often another person's lie. While it is important to discuss public relations from an ethical perspective, it is important to remember that the ethically 'correct' objective is difficult to achieve. This is because the truth is cluttered with ironies and contradictions, some of which have already been described. Chief of these contradictions is that public relations depends on the pre-existence of at least two opposed or competing points of view. If they did not exist, neither would public relations. On top of this unavoidable contradiction society has added another: namely the pursuit of harmony and agreement, of the acceptance of one point of view only. Public relations squirms uncomfortably between these two opposites, and we will look at this in more detail later.

Another problem, meanwhile, is that we want every fragment of communications we hear to be honourable and true. So in our contacts with public relations we are intentionalists: we want an organization's existence to be justified by its virtues, and its actions to be in our best interests. But unfortunately we are consequentialists as well: when we care deeply about something, we are readier to accept that the ends will justify the means taken to achieve it. Public relations cannot always match the universal expectation of fair treatment to our personal opinions about what is right. The contrasts and contradictions can, as we have seen, cause grave errors. They can undermine the noblest communications plan, though practitioners themselves might go to a great deal of trouble to perfect their behaviour. One popular solution is for public relations to adopt a code of ethics. Many professions have these codes, through which 'altruism officially becomes the prime motivator of the profession'.[2] One could, with justification, dismiss the public-relations codes adopted by associations in several countries simply by reminding oneself of the anarchic and unregulated nature of the field. Communications is everywhere and potentially everything: how on earth can it be regulated? It is true that many practitioners want public relations to be seen as a serious 'profession', but how ready are they to submit to the same constrictions as lawyers and accountants, who need years of formal training? Degrees and professional qualifications in public relations are available almost anywhere in the world; but they are not compulsory. Nor, in most cases, need practitioners join the professional associations claiming to represent them. Theoretically, we are all public relations experts.

With all these difficulties, what principles should guide our search for the 'right' way to conduct communications? Are there not absolutes of right and wrong and an absolute truth that we all accept? Perhaps. Sadly, public relations rarely enjoys the luxury of a hard, crystalline division between good and evil. Except perhaps in World War II, public relations has not often presented a monopoly of objective, indisputable rights. As I have, hopefully, made plain by now it is largely a business of creative persuasion, or advocacy, that needs at least one alternative point of view to communicate against. Alternative, and persuasive, truths are easily available, even in the unlikeliest cases. The business of harvesting the planet's oceans provides a second example. A poor country is trying to save its fishing fleet from destruction at the hands of other, richer, nations. This country knows that its isolated fishing communities have nowhere to go if they are bankrupted. It is unable to support the fishermen and their families if their livings are taken away from them. The fishing communities do not enjoy access to the same subsidies, technologies and official expertise existing in western countries. The national government has recently passed new laws freeing resources to improve techniques but for the moment, driven by fear of poverty without hope of welfare support, its people do what they can with limited resources. The loss of the fisheries will also deny the country an important portion of its export income, some of which goes to servicing the debts it owes to the very countries where there is campaigning to stop the fishing. It has to tell its overseas customers and their governments of the disastrous social problem created by preventing the sale of its fish. It is not part of the 'club' of developed nations, it does not understand how to communicate to those customers and governments. It needs public-relations help to establish itself and send its messages. The truth is that it has to launch an expensive international public-relations campaign to prevent misery befalling its citizens.

In Europe and North America, environmentalists are concerned about the cruel and wanton destruction of dolphins tangled in the nets of fleets chasing the same tuna that the dolphins follow. Gruesome pictures and films of dolphins entangled and dying in fishing nets are secretly captured by animal lovers, and snatched up eagerly by the western media, which energetically condemn the ignorant foreigners responsible for such slaughter. An intelligent, friendly, lovable mammal with a special meaning for children and seafarers is being done to death by heartless and greedy fishermen. Conservation groups begin to co-ordinate a public-relations campaign; the pioneers of communicating successfully across the globe about a single problem. Boycotts of the product are organized in several countries, pressure is put on retailers not to purchase tuna from the guilty nation, the retailers in turn put pressure on the buyers to look elsewhere for sources. In parliaments across the western world, concerned environmentalists tap their long-established political connections to obtain an outright import ban. Retailers react by searching for alternative sources of supply and selling only 'dolphin-friendly' labelled tuna; diplomats and international organizations win the right to put monitors on board the tuna fleets of exporting countries. The truth is that the secret of dolphin deaths has escaped, and it is simply unacceptable to western consumers, children, retailers, activists and the politicians representing them.

WHICH MESSAGE IS 'TRUE'?

'Life suggests that truth-telling is difficult stuff, at best a dim shadowing of maybes and oughts. Figuring out the truth becomes a guessing game, because the sources that claim to be giving all these facts can rarely be trusted.'[3] But even if two opposed messages are trustworthy, the *absolute truth* of one over the other is tough to decide once an audience has – as in the case just outlined – closely examined all the information communicated to it. So in spite of being responsible for packaging solid and accurate information, public relations has a dubious reputation. Dubious, as there is a contradiction in its relationship to the truth. Public relations may never lie, but the purest practitioner and the most sacred source depends, as we mentioned, on the existence of more than one 'truth': of an alternative model, product, organization, view, way of life, whose supporters struggle for the same audience. In order to make a living, practitioners need the existence of that alternative, 'untrue' communications to oppose their own 'truth'. Public relations then aids all sides in the communications struggle. Everyone is convinced – publicly at least – of the sincerity and truthfulness of their respective cases. In the end, the ideal outcome of the contest between alternative ideas about what is 'right' – the 'right' breakfast cereal to eat, the 'right' company to buy shares in, the 'right' party to vote for, the 'right' side of an issue to support – is victory for one message. The acceptance of one side's messages over its opponents, of one view and one organization as 'correct' and the others as 'incorrect'. Once the 'correct' view has been accepted, it buckles on the armour of an unchangeable 'truth'. It becomes an 'objective' opinion shared by all rather than a 'subjective' opinion put about by one side only. In the ideal outcome, the communications war ends. Complete victory for a message over its rivals is the impossible goal of almost everybody engaged in public relations.

We concentrate on that message too much in our contradictory search for objective truth and personal victory, and in the process arrive at unjust conclusions about public relations. The reason for this misjudgement is that the message is the root of the public-relations effort. We are encouraged by public-relations practitioners to make a judgement about an issue based on which message is right and which is wrong – and by others to make a judgement about the right of public relations to dress up the deadliest message and make it beautiful. Certainly, practitioners are paid to clean messages until they glow with virtue and are free from the contaminants of faulty logic, slipshod presentation and insufficient ethical detail. The task is large, because 'It is no longer good enough for an organisation to say they "are" this or that,' warns one author, 'they must now articulate what they "do" and how they do what they "do".'[4] That being said, those contaminants are hard to expel from messages, and perhaps we would learn more by looking at them rather than at the message itself. Although they take much of the blame for the shortcomings of public relations, it must also be said that they are redeeming flaws – and without flaws, as the painter Degas argued, there is no life.

The first flaw, obviously present in every public-relations message, is that it inevitably reflects the prejudices of the sender. This prejudice guarantees that however much trouble is taken to get a message across, certain people will never be able to accept it. Messages are products of division. If we were flawless and without prejudice, we would not need to communicate. We would not need to coax audiences over to our product and away from someone else's; to our ideas and away from someone else's; to our cause and away from someone else's; to a commitment and away from apathy or disbelief or non-involvement. A message is inevitably flawed because it implies the existence of an unbeatable alternative. To take an extreme case, the public-relations director of a European cosmetics company involved in animal experiments may be plucky enough to make contact on this issue with consumer groups, journalists and politicians interested in the problem. This pool of experts embodies public opinion and is likely to be respected by consumers for their 'objectivity'. It is therefore reasonable for that cosmetics company to turn to them with a communications programme about its research into alternatives to animal testing, arguing the need for safety testing on medical grounds, delivering these messages by trained company spokespeople, creating a regular publication giving information on alternative research and presenting its position in a series of advertisements in trade magazines. The company might do all of these things, but it is of course biased and will never convince those equally biased activists who care so much about the issue that they are even prepared to free laboratory animals, threaten scientists and destroy their property. The shock tactics of British animal-rights groups have successfully generated publicity and raised awareness. Their unlawful activities have inspired other efforts, imaginative and legal: dramatic footage of animal laboratories for public consumption; powerful, uncompromising and persuasive literature, especially as far as younger audiences are concerned; a well-established series of contacts in the media and politics.

A second redeeming flaw is that a message is always affected by the moment of its release. Good and bad timing are possible, but not perfect timing. In 1989, a national office of an international company showed good timing when it decided its sponsorship programme was spread over too many worthy and well-known causes. The corporation itself did not benefit from the large sums it distributed. It decided to rectify this by concentrating on one particular cause – the environment. A concentration of resources, it felt, would clearly associate the corporation with one special issue to the advantage of both. It was interested in a cause that would appeal to the young. Up to then, the branch's country had not taken a strong interest in environmental matters. It was not a high priority with the local media. But executives felt that the concern elsewhere in the world would eventually make an impact. They decided to anticipate this by developing a 'green' programme in advance, sensibly built around a well-known, much-loved, national park. The corporation sponsored a trail map to coincide with the park's anniversary. It sponsored a television documentary on the park, began to pioneer the local use of recycled stationery and developed a 'green' logo for use on all the relevant materials it produced. The media were more than ready to take an interest in the park, and in a briefing were introduced to the corporation's plans for it along with their wider environmental ambitions. Young potential customers were introduced to the programme through television and press advertising and a direct mail shot was made to existing customers. Early action, and early association with a single issue, enabled the corporation to establish useful links with environmental officials in anticipation of future initiatives, and ultimately turned the corporation into a leading national commentator on the environment.

Bad timing ensured two different fates for the same message in the hands of the same people. Conservative Party election managers campaigned under the message 'Tranquility' in 1922. It had a strong appeal for electors, who felt that a steady hand was required to lead the country through a period of depression. The message was churned out in all literature, on posters and in campaign speeches. It reflected the mood of the times and helped the Conservatives win a handsome victory, 'but when Baldwin repeated it in 1929, under the title "Safety First", it proved a great flop', recalled Harold Macmillan.[5] Party managers tried to strike exactly the same chords of security and steadiness that 'Tranquility' had struck seven years previously. The message was similar, it was supported by the most sophisticated campaign office in the country. Few in the Party anticipated defeat, yet defeated they were because now voters had changed their minds. They were in no mood for tranquility or 'Safety First'. 'It reflected a tired and rather defeatist mood', Macmillan considered. 'Torpid, sleepy, barren,' Lloyd George now called the Government that had once made a virtue of 'Tranquility' to defeat him in 1922.[6] The electorate agreed. Now they wanted action to pull the country out of its economic difficulties, but 'There was no call to positive or creative action.'[7] Same message, same audience. Different time, different perception, different result.

A third flaw, adulterating the impact of any message – even when it is factual and apparently unanswerable – is the vehicle chosen for its delivery. The format, the event, the document selected is a source of extraneous 'noise' that supplements and distorts the message itself. The vehicle has its own rules – perhaps set by the design, or the words, and these priorities help decide how the message is received. In the 1930s, the increase in cars and in car accidents prompted the British Government to launch a road safety information campaign. A dramatic poster was designed to put the message of safe driving across. It was the head and shoulders of a grieving widow, veiled and dressed in black. The method of delivery was so overpowering that the public ignored the poster's actual, unarguable, message, and instead complained it was too depressing to look at. The poster was withdrawn.

The unavoidable presence of flaws in any communications plan undermines its chance of total success. Even if a communicator or an audience is capable of bestowing on any message the priceless gift of 'objectivity', the physical processes that go into its preparation 'pollute' the process, make it subjective and ensure the existence of a debate. Because a message cannot exist as a thought and must be converted into something, it is possible for competing messages to cast doubt on it, to question it by presenting alternatives. Messages are not prepared in the sterile environment of a laboratory. They cannot distil the contradictions of an emotion or problem into an irrefutable equation. They are imperfect, by their very nature, because they are made by and must deal with human beings. Messages remain the bruised fruit of these imperfections, for all the advances in transmission that allow them to reach us instantly, at any moment of the communicator's choosing, and for all the forms of expression now available. Victory is rarely achieved unless opponents run out of money, ideas, legal rights of self-expression, or morale. This is fortunate, because the problem with unconditional and guaranteed victory for public relations is that it would automatically end the necessity to communicate, and to employ experts in communication. Without opposition there would be nothing to say, apart perhaps from unopposed campaigns that become more strident and less creative in order to perpetuate belief – in other words, propaganda.

Perhaps that is where we have been mistaken. That difference between propaganda and a choice of communications has been set by society as a characteristic of freedom. It is the difference between Napoleon the media-suppressing Emperor, and the image of liberty's champion carefully promoted by him in final exile and still swallowed by large numbers of Europeans. We can look back at the end of the twentieth century and wonder if this was a mistake. There are so many ways of delivery that we have difficulty separating truth from untruth. Lost in a flood of communications, we the blinded audience can only turn to 'the stock of commonplaces, prejudices, fag-ends of ideas or simply empty words which chance has piled up in [our] mind'.[8] Among those terrible simplicities is an honourable but misleading desire *for* simplicity, for all issues to be boiled down to their bare bones, reduced to a simple matter of right and wrong. Cuba wrong. Recycling right. Union Carbide wrong.

It has often been said that we need God to regulate our moral sensibility. Without God we struggle to distinguish between absolutes of right and wrong on the rare occasions they really do arise. Worse, we struggle to identify attempts at dialogue and at control. This is a much more common and serious event. How can we differentiate the two in this time of relative, 'godless', communications? The expansion of our physical world through communications is responsible for our diminished spiritual world. Yes, it would be wrong to neglect the consolations, the chance to engage in the wider world of ideas that public relations has offered. A great opportunity, though, has also been missed. Until recent times, the architecture of our ancestors' minds was subject to physical limits on time and space, but there was compensation because in many areas of their lives their services or beliefs were not required. Institutions were smaller, poorer, and restricted to a glittering circle of participants. This was free space, the realm of personal speculation and play. Now organizations do not feel comfortable about that unfilled space. They use public relations to talk with us, or at us. They compete to make their message the conventional wisdom. More orthodoxy is, without doubt, required from us today than at the height of the Spanish Inquisition.

One may ask whether this invasion of our free space has passed a critical point, when the law of diminishing returns sets in. The brevity of fame and fashion, of attention spans, and the well-documented reduction of sound into bite-size portions may suggest that it has. There is too much of everything. Our free space is cluttered: where do we stand on this or that issue? How many plain truths are we told by the media to confront? Where is dialogue here? Too much public relations demands that we take a stand for its clients. Taking a stand, making a judgement, seems the democratic thing to do. Thank goodness for it. Surely we are right to solve a dilemma by a fragmentary and erratic process of personal judgement – the ghost of an expired religiosity. It is less easy for us to examine communications from the perspective of dialogue versus control. The emotions they raise are far more unsettling and personal than those involved in taking sides on a particular issue. A movement of the thumbs up or down is easier than contemplating the means by which the decisive message was actually delivered to you. Universal communications has not created a better informed audience. Nor, we can now see is an open, communicating society the main measure of freedom. How will organizations conduct their future public relations as we take advantage of the renewed free space that information technology is creating for us? The population of rural counties in America is growing again because our wired citizens are taking to the hills to conduct their business. Is this an opportunity for dialogue between scattered audiences and organizations, or will the physical dispersion of that same audience intensify the choice of messages and further erode our capacity for reflection? It is not a problem of big versus small government, or right or wrong, but of volume and variety – the rudiments of free speech.

WHAT IS DIALOGUE?

Given the magnitude of the problem, the attempt of public relations to achieve dialogue has been insufficient. One method has been to reach the community through increased social responsibility. The result is patchy, anywhere between the corporate fund-raising drives and sponsorship of national parks previously described. In spite of this, there has been a great deal of high-minded and mistaken ethical comment about completely changing an organization's fundamental messages and practices to reflect wishy-washy notions about doing good. 'There is a growing coalition between the study of corporate social responsibility and business ethics.'[9] Intertwined, the two have made a serious impact on public relations. A Norwegian academic, Geir Vestheim, identified three contradictions confronting us when exposed to public-relations rhetoric as individuals in our own right, as citizens in the community and as customers and consumers of goods. Much of the criticism of public relations, he notes, is made by people who momentarily fasten on to one or other of the three perceptions, but do not see that the real problem is the contrary tensions produced by all three acting together in their response to a message. Vestheim's solution is to advocate a new public rhetoric, which is already in transition from the purely commercial language of business and embraces elements of social conscience, politics, non-government and commercial organizations. The key, he asserts, is the unbusinesslike language now being developed in public relations rhetoric. We should, he argues, rope it to classical rhetorical theory, which even in the ancient world 'was defined as the art of using speech to persuade, influence and please the audience in such a way that certain viewpoints or attitudes were accepted'.[10]

This idea already forms the basis for many socially responsible public-relations programmes, including the Co-op Bank's ethical investment policy. The rhetoric of good intent is apparently expected to show that businesses are prepared to don the purple of responsible corporate citizenship. 'We at Arkansas Power & Light Company have made a multimillion dollar commitment to the growth and prosperity of our state. We call it "Teamwork Arkansas",' writes the president of the company in the foreword to 'Arkansas', a report 'on life in Arkansas' prepared by the company's office on economic development. AP&L's 'Teamwork Arkansas' was introduced in the 1980s to do just about everything a government might think of doing for itself. Teamwork 'aggressively promotes expansion of existing industry, attraction of new industry from around the world and assistance for local communities whose growth we encourage'.[11] The twofold public relations purpose: to attract investment, and to demonstrate AP&L's commitment to citizens of the State, reflects the social responsibility displayed by many corporations, matching Vestheim's arguments for an uncommercial element in commercial communications so that corporations will meet their public on a more equal footing. AP&L, for instance, is very concerned about education reform and works with 'the Arkansas Business Council Foundation, a non-profit organization made up of the most influential businessmen in the State.'[12]

Other organizations prefer an even more radical approach to their commercial and societal responsibilities, and even sacrifice the former to the latter. When the authors of *The 100 Best Companies to Work for in America*, were considering which companies to include in the new edition of their book they received a letter from the socially aware Vermont ice-cream maker Ben & Jerry's Homemade Inc. The company's director of 'social missions' asked to be left out as the company felt it had too much to learn itself, and would not be ready to give advice to other businesses. The public relations here has modelled itself on the lines of responsible rhetoric. Instead of 'we're too busy to handle non-business calls' Ben & Jerry's said, 'we're human. We've got a lot to learn too.' It was a moment of rare and healthy humility. A corporation that prefers not to be in a book for which, as one newspaper put it: 'Many companies would kill to get included.'[13]

Yet this approach to openness and dialogue has its critics. A successful businesswoman made her feelings about social responsiblity plain in the novel *Atlas Shrugged*:

> She stopped and looked down at the magazines on the coffee table. Their headlines said: 'The new social conscience,' 'Our Duty to the Underprivileged,' 'Need versus Greed.' With a single movement of her arm, the abrupt, explosive movement of sheer physical brutality, such as he had never seen from her before, she swept the magazines off the table and went on, her voice reciting a list of figures without a break, as if there were no connection between her mind and the violence of her body.[14]

Public relations and social virtue, it should quickly be conceded, have a good deal to offer each other. A limited exploration of social responsibility will heighten public relations' understanding of itself, and definitely increase the power it already wields. Quite possibly, a continuous and publicly communicated effort by practitioners to address the place of ethics in their work will convince anyone unable to see merit or scruples in public relations. At the same time, there is a danger of death by social responsibility. Some of the imperfections in public relations are, I have tried to argue, signs of healthy life. The continued search for ethically sound dialogue through the rhetoric of the good corporate citizen and the promise of two-way communications raises our expectations but neglects the facts about the imbalance organizations and audiences always have in relation to each other. They play different parts in a public-relations strategy, where one is always stronger than the other – yet those realities are not properly addressed by diverting resources into socially responsible activities. Important and worthwhile as these activities often appear, they slow the pace at which goods and services can be provided for us. Funnelling increased money into 'pretend communications' also increases the intrusiveness of organizations under the guise of dialogue, and impinges upon our remaining free space. If there is a fundamental danger in the work of public relations, it does not lie in its occasional abuses of ethics – which are relatively easy to identify. It lies in its random use of socially responsible rhetoric to expand its work and justify its status to the point where it swallows time and budgets in meaningless and unproductive exercises. For every praised and justified exercise in open dialogue, a pointless act of 'socially responsible' public relations trails uselessly in its wake.

> We've got the most modern plant in the country and the best organization. That seems to me to be an indisputable fact, because we got the Industrial Efficiency Award of Globe Magazine last year. So

we can maintain that we've done our best and nobody can blame us. But we cannot help it if the iron ore situation is a national problem. We could not get the ore, Jim.[15]

In the search for ethical respectability for themselves and their clients, public relations practitioners have largely overlooked the need for contradictions to exist in their work. Those who believe public relations cannot provide true clarity miss the same point. Both sides try to solve this 'problem' by ethical overkill – seeking a winning message, a socially responsible means of communications, or intrusive control in the sheep's clothing of 'dialogue'. They ignore the alternative interpretation: that the flaws and contradictions in public relations are not impediments to the purity of a message, but signs of its life, health and vigour. The inescapable flaws in the most carefully constructed message ensure it will be rejected by some and subscribed to by others. Communications must divide and advocate one side above another. By doing so, it perpetuates choice, and choices are manifestations of free societies. Proper public-relations dialogue is an imperfect, friendly, energetic, open and frank exchange of biased viewpoints. Far better for public relations to celebrate its diversity and subjectivity. It presages a world opened to dialogue, where the views of the smallest audience matters to the biggest corporation, and where the humblest person has the capacity to move mountains.

NOTES

1 Sampson, Anthony. 'The anatomy of publicity'. *Spectator*, 7 November 1992.
2 Buchholz, William J. 'Deciphering professional codes of ethics'. *IEEE Transactions on Professional Communication*, vol 32, no. 2 (2 June 1989) p 62.
3 Ibid., p 66.
4 McIntosh, Malcolm *et al. Good Business? Case Studies in Corporate Social Responsibility*. (Bristol, UK: SAUS Publications, 1993) p 2.
5 Macmillan, Harold. *Winds of Change* (London: Macmillan, 1966) p 131.
6 Young, G.M. *Stanley Baldwin* (London: Rupert Hart-Davis, 1952) p 139.
7 Ibid., p 244.
8 Ortega y Gasset, José. *The Revolt of the Masses* (New York: Norton, 1957. First published in 1930) p 70.
9 McIntosh. *Good Business?*, p 6.
10 Vestheim, Geir. Senior Researcher, Eastern Norway Research Institute. 'Rhetorical theory: issues for public relations'. CERP-Education Spring Conference paper, London, June 1992, p 2.
11 'Arkansas'. *A Report from the Arkansas Power & Light Company's Office of Economic Development on Life in Arkansas*. Undated.
12 Ibid.
13 *The Globe & Mail* (Toronto, Canada), 21 March 1994 Section B, p B4.
14 Rand, Ayn. *Atlas Shrugged* (New York: Signet, 1957) p 590.
15 Ibid., p 49.

CHAPTER ELEVEN

Liberation by Exchange

Do not regard it as your task, and do not bring any
pressure to bear on the peoples, to change their manners,
customs, and uses, unless they are evidently contrary to
religion and sound morals.[1]

The Sacred Congregation for the Propagation of the Faith (the Propaganda).
Instructions to vicars apostolic in overseas missions,1659

The missionary organization that gave us the totalitarian word 'propaganda' in fact preached tolerance of peoples and cultures. 'What could be more absurd', the Propaganda argued, 'than to transport France, Spain, Italy, or some other European country to China? Do not introduce all that to them, but only the Faith, which does not despise or destroy the manners and customs of any people, always supposing that they are not evil, but rather wishes to see them preserved unharmed.'[2] Respect your audience and concentrate on the message alone. These are things later propagandists forgot, and many internationally minded corporations have still to learn. The Propaganda was an early communicator on a global scale and international public relations will not find better advice than theirs:

> It is the nature of men to love and treasure above everything else their own country and that which belongs to it; in consequence there is no stronger cause for alienation and hate than an attack on local customs, especially when these go back to a venerable antiquity. This is more especially the case, when an attempt is made to introduce the customs of another people in place of those which have been abolished. Do not draw invidious contrasts between the customs of the peoples and those of Europe; do your utmost to adapt yourselves to them.[3]

Organizations failing to take this good communications advice are not difficult to find. Euro-Disney, California's re-export of European folk history, was in trouble well before opening day. French critics described it as a cultural Chernobyl, even though the facility was legally bound to respect local culture. The hype created for the Paris announcement of Euro-Disney's share price did not save Mickey Mouse and Disney's Chief Executive

Michael Eisner from being pelted with eggs, tomato sauce, and cries of 'Mickey go home'. Lack of cultural awareness hurt the project. According to one account, a visiting Disney executive from the States noticed a Mercedes parked outside one of the cheaper-range hotels on the site. Mercedes drivers, he yelled at local marketing managers, belong in the expensive hotels. He did not know that Mercedes 190s are quite commonplace in Europe, and not the cars of the well-to-do. French employees welcomed the first-name corporate structure, but were less keen to cut hair or trim nails to Disney regulations. Disney did not understand that in Europe people tend to eat at set times. The all-day American-style hot dog stalls were unpatronized as customers descended on the restaurants at the same moment. To top it all, Euro-Disney's restaurants did not serve alcohol at lunch. No wine in France? *Newsweek* lambasted the ignorance behind the entire enterprise.

> 'I'm not sure the Europeans will stand in line in winter,' ventured one executive at a strategy meeting. 'The answer' . . . recounts a former Disney executive, was: 'The Japanese do.' No one said, 'The Japanese are different.'[4]

Two wiser and equally American symbols of popular culture, Coke and Pepsi, ensured that their international bottling operations were locally owned, making them two of the few organizations sensible enough to profit from the Propaganda's main recommendation. Local ownership stimulates local investment capital and reduces the possibility of take-overs by xenophobic governments. 'He speaks the language,' said a Coke official of its typical overseas bottler, 'knows the culture, and understands the local laws.' That decentralization helps both companies adapt their sophisticated marketing skills to prevailing cultural institutions. 'We're not multinational, we're multilocal,' another executive once commented.[5]

The task of infiltrating community boundaries, whether international or domestic, has profoundly affected communications. Because of it, public relations has managed to outgrow its national origins and assume larger and sophisticated responsibilities. Entire countries and cultures are forming intricate connections as methods of business, or other activities are introduced from one to the other. In the crucible of activities and ideas, national identities are by-passed to market services to customers who at another level are often worried that the international goods and services they themselves demand will undermine their cultural identity. Public relations plays a helpful, central role in smoothing that process of change. It works inside and outside of cultural boundaries, respecting old customs while conveying the exciting possibilities of new ones. Better knowledge of public relations has also enabled newcomers to observe and mimic its techniques, and add their fresh, freed voices to the interplay of structured communications.

Communities are able to enter the external communications process for the first time, and to shape messages with public relations. Always shifting and never entirely stable, the flood of messages and responses presents fertile international opportunities for professional communicators, and forces all to re-examine our culturally defined views about right and wrong, truth and untruth, open and secretiveness. Public relations can serve as a vessel for understanding.

Public relations and communities were thrown together in the nineteenth century by the rapid growth of industry. New loyalties were needed by the people concentrated in workplaces or large housing developments. Scattered, stable, inert, small village settlements were replaced by concentrated, volatile, mobile masses of city dwellers, technologically alert, assisted by advances in education, dependent on manufacturers to supply them with goods and on politicians for improvements to their working and living conditions. It was necessary for suppliers of goods and services to compete. Advertisements multiplied. Horse-drawn sign vans helped slow traffic, and 'advertising men paced the streets, frequently in lines, carrying banners on sandwich boards fore and aft, proclaiming the merits of every conceivable article of merchandise'.[6] Others trudged along inside models of the company symbol or product: boots, tea caddies, blacking. A colourful period of development in commercial communications was inaugurated by businesses that left other organizations behind. 'The reason that preachers in this present generation are less successful in getting people to want goodness than business men are in getting them to want motor cars, hats and pianolas,' speculated an early twentieth-century writer excited by the social impact of business, 'is that business men as a class are more close and desperate students of human nature, and have boned down harder to the art of touching the imaginations of crowds.'[7] This intensification in public communications was partly inspired by the newspapers, able to circulate among millions of readers through advances in printing technology. Modern public relations owes much to the rotary press which accelerated the printing process in the 1840s; and stereotyping – the introduction from the 1850s of simultaneous printing on both sides of paper. The faster printing machines could send people detailed communications – information and points of view on apparently important matters that formerly would have been contemplated by a privileged few. The arrival of a news-hungry press presented publicity opportunities to organizations interested in shaping that news. A few people saw the consequences of this for the media:

> The old village or small town way of sending out enterprising young men to gather up the news in the community has become impracticable, and the publicity agent, representing certain great interests, certain great corporations, which may be commercial

organizations, academic corporations, or otherwise, has become possibly a necessity of our modern life.[8]

These were the glory days of the publicist, the first sub-specialists in public relations, depicted as Kenneth Escott and Howard Littlefield Ph.D in *Babbit*, Sinclair Lewis's satire of the roaring twenties in America.

> [Littlefield] could, at ten hours' notice, appear before the board of aldermen or the state legislature and prove, absolutely, with figures all in rows and with precedents from Poland and New Zealand, that the street-car company loved the Public and yearned over its employees; that all its stock was owned by Widows and Orphans; and that whatever it desired to do would benefit property-owners by increasing rental values, and help the poor by lowering rents.[9]

Photographic and film processes had improved on the strength of the image to move people, and shaped the ability of public relations to be conscious of events and pictures as much as of words and figures. We readily project stock images onto what we read. In other words, the message of the image has even penetrated our perception of written communications.

Publicists saw that they could use all these media to carry messages to millions of people. They hurried to cultivate links with journalists, and the closer the better. The new contract between organizations, media and the industrial community offered readers once unavailable information, but choked off exclusively local eccentricities and opinions in favour of a commonly shared, carefully constructed, standard and insecure conventional wisdom. In this connection, we mourn small publications like the *Westport Mirror*, Canada's oldest newspaper, which finally closed in 1993, defeated by the cost of serving a population of less than seven hundred. It marks the end of a century-old consolidation towards cultural homogeneity led by the western world. It may be, though, that advances in technology will soon start returning to the small-world communicators the power and influence that the big machines steadily stripped from them. If that is the case, autonomous papers such as the *Mirror* will be reborn in a different form, and force a change in traditional, media-dominated patterns of public relations.

One signal that rebirth may be imminent is that business communications between organizations and peoples internationally have blossomed into a global connectedness between ideas and cultures. Early observers of these trends believed they proved the newly-developed principle of evolution as manufacturers and nations strove to supply people with industrial goods and compete with each other. Competition between modern civilizations, according to the influential nineteenth-century Scottish philosopher David George Ritchie, took place primarily between groups and races. This was demonstrated by the economic rivalry between Britain and America. As the protagonists in this commercial competition manoeuvred for position, Ritchie anticipated that industrial competition – and consequently communication – would enlarge into a struggle between the ideas, customs, laws and beliefs of non-commercial institutions: 'Natural selection does not cease to operate, but the conflict of ideas takes the place of the competition of animal organisms.'[10] He felt that this transition would occur initially as a 'spontaneous variation', but as civilizations progressed and languages grew increasingly sophisticated, this sign of evolution would be guided by 'deliberate reflection',[11] which has come about through the conduit of public relations. Ritchie also declared that knowing *how* deliberate reflection appeared was unnecessary, but conceded that changes in language and social institutions were turning the latter into vehicles for the communication of experience. This advance beyond the mere provision of goods and services enabled institutions to wield greater control over the evolution of society.[12] Ritchie's prognosis pre-dates the modern trend towards the global expansion of 'deliberate reflection'. He was not able to see the revolution in information technology that currently realizes the capacity of public relations to 'deliberately reflect' to the public.

Alongside these changes is one that was not anticipated – better access to a commonly understood 'language' of words and symbols that we can all partly understand. This language, standardized by public relations and the media, enables formerly impotent and isolated communities to participate in the reflective process. Because of public relations, a leading journalist once recorded, money was not the sole factor in deciding whether or not a point of view received a hearing. Energy, imagination and judgement can put 'a low budget public relations office, representing a small business, a college, a church group, or a philanthropy, on a par with the most powerful organisation'.[13] The liberation of communities through public relations not only changes their relations with external organizations. It also changes the role of the individual within a community, and a community's definition of itself.

Our identities are inextricably woven into the act of communications, which we share with growing numbers of people. Identities are influenced by relationships, relationships are shaped by the contacts and communications we make, and science is constantly seeking new ways of bringing us into contact with people of whose existence we may not have even been aware – the mutual, inextricable bond between technology, public relations, liberty, and human contact. This is evident in all sorts of undramatic yet telling ways. I am listening to the news on the radio. The newsreader announces a decision by the Metro Toronto Schools Board to accept over a million dollars from PepsiCo Canada. Pepsi has arranged to fund a school lunch programme and set up drinks machines in the school. A school pupil, Sarah Elliot, objects and has formed a protest group. She is interviewed, and argues that it is the beginning of corporate control of the school curriculum, and that Pepsi is simply interested in hooking young people on to what some have labelled a nutritionally weak drink. She makes her case well and with enthusiasm. She is thoroughly at home with the electronic media, perhaps from having been exposed to it from birth. The announcer turns to the president and CEO of PepsiCo Canada, who responds that Pepsi has no curricular interests and merely wants to support the Board's $1.4 million lunch-funding target and to install vending machines. Ninety per cent of students interviewed by an independent research firm, he reveals, liked educational partnerships with industry and with Pepsi in particular. Lastly, he argues that Pepsi is not restricting choice, as milk and drinking fountains are available to students. The Metro Toronto School Board, he says, simply took the opportunity to help fund a school-meals programme, providing convenience for lunch and needed finance. Sarah responds by introducing a wider problem she has with the company's involvement in education. Many students, she claims, are uncomfortable with Pepsi's political affiliations – Pepsi has investments in Myanmar (Burma), where its bottling partner company has close ties to the repressive military dictatorship. PepsiCo's position is that it does not support political parties, rather the welfare of local people in over 150 countries. Sarah remains unconvinced, and has prepared a presentation to deliver to the School Board. The founding fathers of Pepsi would probably not have considered sending a senior executive to justify matters of business policy to a high school student in a public debate at peak listening hours. Such opportunities are now important, and public relations must be able to spot them. The media coverage Sarah has achieved, and her presentation to the School Board, hinges on her instinct for public relations. She communicates effectively, is taken seriously, and is able to present her case to large and influential audiences. Her 'low-budget public relations' is for the moment as effective as PepsiCo's high-budget alternative.

The liberating capability of low-budget public relations is even clearer on an international scale. Technology can penetrate the dark, empty segments of our planet, reaches into them, extracts news it feels to be important or interesting, and sends it to teeming, distant settlements in opposite parts of the earth. International public relations has flourished amid these developments although it has a longer, if erratic, history. In addition to the powerful Propaganda, less well funded efforts have occasionally been made to publicly communicate across cultural or political borders. Keen to introduce the world to the exciting possibilities of the industrial age, the poet Shelley had the inspired idea of instructing mankind in political rights and scientific progress by attaching little messages to hand-stitched silk balloons – the poet was one of the first people to experiment with balloons and helium – then floating them off in various parts of Europe during the early 1800s. Modern public relations does not have to send balloons into the void, carrying unheard-of messages to complete strangers: it can rely on the fact that increasing contact and communication has constructed a shared perceptual map so that corporations can learn to navigate across borders.

In the early 1990s, a multinational corporation purchased a redundant rare earth plant in a rural district of a south-east Asian country. The previous owners and several nearby industries had suffered bad publicity and opposition, and the whole area was highly sensitive to the prospect of a new arrival. Environmentally conscious residents were alert to the threat of exploitation, and had made their case to the media. Lacking experience at dialogue with intruding organizations from other cultures, the residents employed passionate, one-way, but quite effective means of expression. A Japanese company mining in the same area faced threats, stonings and demonstrations. The environment ministry was not keen, on the strength of this, to re-activate the plant. But by working with a local consultancy, the multi-national managed to open discussions with the community by applying a programme that contained three elements:

- Preparedness. A communications package recognizing that the corporation would sometimes be forced to react, and react in a uniform way, to difficult questions and criticism. The package contained 'Q&As' (Questions and Answers) designed to include consistent responses to the most difficult anticipated questions; and fact sheets with basic background information on the corporation and the issue, for distribution to inquirers.

- Media relations. An attempt was made to communicate openly with the press about the company's plans. A tour of the corporation's facilities was arranged, a 'getting to know you' press dinner was held, and of course a series of news releases was prepared.

- Community relations. The future of the rare earth facility depended on the ability of the corporation to win trust from a distrustful community. A site-visit programme was established for local leaders and government officials. At all times, the company took great care to present its views in an 'objective' and unemotional manner to residents and media.

The local consultancy prepared a factual report on meetings the corporation had held with community leaders. It was then used as a substitute for a survey of residents' feelings towards the plant's start-up. Its findings were crucial, as the final meeting of the ministerial approval board concentrated heavily on it to assess local fears. Eventually, verbal permission was given to re-start the plant.

People do not simply absorb external messages: they have the power to answer back and to take action, to respond if they feel their views are not being recognized. Communications, by giving audiences the power to speak, endows them with the power to express their distinctiveness – joyfully, aggressively, maybe threateningly. Global public relations, developed as a business to serve commercial operations, is broadening into a powerful non-commercial force. Sometimes it uses the written word to connect us to each other; sometimes it uses the spoken word or visualized messages; it moulds messages around ideas and helps us to persuade, to inform, to meet people we would once never have known, but who now matter to us.[14] A starving child from a hungry, distant continent was not our great-great-grandparents' problem because they did not know her. Now, she visits our home every night and forces us to react by switching channels or coming to her aid. Press officers for famine-relief organizations need to show the camera where she and millions like her can be found, to motivate their donors. Communicators like them help her to find a space in the wider world: one day soon, she will find her own voice.

NOTES

1 Neill, Steven, *A History of Christian Missions* (London: Penguin, 1986. 2nd edition) p 153.
2 Ibid.
3 Ibid.
4 'Mickey's trip to trouble'. *Newsweek,* 14 February 1994.
5 Louis, J. C. and Yazijian, H. *The Cola Wars* (New York: Everest House, 1980) p 153.
6 Dodds, John W. *The Age of Paradox. A biography of England, 1841–51* (London: Gollancz, 1953) p 410.
7 Lee, Gerald Stanley. *Crowds. A study of the genius of democracy and of the fears, desires and expectations of the people* (Toronto: Briggs, 1913) p 135.
8 Lee, Ivy. *Publicity: some of the things it is and is not* (New York: Industries Publishing, 1925) p 30.
9 Lewis, Sinclair. *Babbit* (New York: Grosset & Dunlap, 1922) p 25.
10 Ritchie, David George. *Darwinism and Politics* (London, 1891. 2nd edition) p 100.
11 Ibid., p 99.
12 Ibid., p 26.
13 *Encyclopaedia Britannica* (1960) p 744. From the late 1920s to the 1960s, public relations was considered significant enough to deserve a large entry in the Encyclopaedia. The 1960 Encyclopaedia devoted eight columns to the topic, indicating its importance, written by Joseph Anthony, an editor and journalist.
14 For general guidance on how to communicate, all public-relations practitioners should remember Lord Chesterfield's advice to his son: 'You cannot but be convinced that a man who speaks and writes with elegance and grace; who makes choice of good words, and adorns and embellishes the subject upon which he either speaks or writes, will persuade better, and succeed more easily in obtaining what he wishes, than a man who does not explain himself clearly; speaks his language ill; or makes use of low and vulgar expressions; and who has neither grace nor elegance in any thing that he says.' *Chesterfield's Letters to his Son* (New York: Dodge, *c.* 1915) p 9.

CHAPTER TWELVE

'The Ringing Grooves of Change'

Prepare to leave your idea of audience behind.[1]

Interactive Media Festival advertisement

Kate Haswell presented the news for Westcountry television in south-west England. She became one of the new channel's top presenters on its six o'clock flagship programme. Her face was familiar to us during 1992 and 1993. In August of that year we travelled to Toronto, Canada, where there are well over 40 television channels. One evening that winter, I was watching CBC Newsworld, a 24-hour Canadian station that broadcasts twenty minutes of the BBC's World Service television news on the prime half hours and deep into the night. It is popular: British accents and extensive international content lend it a certain cachet. That evening, the news reader looked out of place in the corner of our room. I felt rather disembodied when I finally registered Kate Haswell, now presenting the news to a Canadian audience. The following April we returned to Britain. Thirty thousand feet over the Atlantic I again met Kate, courtesy of British Airways' contract with the BBC to screen World Service News for passengers. Two points arise from this: first, it is often easier to receive than to avoid detailed and instant communications from the rest of the world; second, that all this scattered information can be flashed from country to country, by a single organization embodied by a single person. We might agree with Marx that the effects of this latest step in the 'constant revolutionising of production' will plunge the world into a new round of drastic change:

> All fixed, fast frozen relations, with their train of ancient and venerable prejudices and opinions, are swept away, all new formed ones become antiquated before they can ossify. All that is solid melts into the air, all that is holy is profaned, and man is at last compelled to face with sober senses, his real conditions of life, and his relations with his kind.[2]

We cannot escape the communicators; and given that, do we, the audience, have the right to guide what they choose to say to us? Are we in fact already doing so? In the near future it is highly likely that the communicators will leave our newspapers, radios and television screens, and closely involve themselves in other aspects of our lives.

One more press conference. The international media director for Greenpeace is seated at a conference table in Vancouver, delivering her organization's messages on nuclear waste dumping in the North Atlantic and outlining a forthcoming summer programme of high-profile demonstrations. Around the table is her audience – environmental correspondents from western Europe and North America. The exact same people are simultaneously asking questions from offices in their own countries. In Vancouver, they are moving, life-size, transmitted holographic images.

The latest restructuring plans were completed, and had to be explained to the corporation's employees. Instead of a mass meeting, a departmental briefing and articles in the company magazine, the communications director mailed a specially prepared virtual reality programme to employees in their homes. Through visors and body sensors, they saw and felt the detail of the changes. In the programme, they walked through the ideal post-change department and its flawed pre-change counterpart. They were ushered into the president's office and by interrupting her programmed talk, were able to ask questions about the changes. At the end of the programme, the restructuring was represented as a giant matrix, which could be viewed from a distance or approached, entered and explored down to the level of every individual employee.

Much public discussion has naturally concerned the exciting uses to which the new technology will be put: the opportunity for student doctors to practise operations, for architects to plan and tour entire cyberspace cities, for interactive games, for interactive sex or violence, for trainee pilots, for tourists to visit distant countries without leaving their homes, for university courses. But what are the implications for public relations? They will, we suspect, enlarge the range of communications tools and require one or two practical changes in the nature of everyday work. Over the next generation, there will be a remarkable evolution in human affairs, and this will affect what public relations does, what it says and to whom. We must try to sketch, as best we can, the world that the coming generations of practitioners must deal with. It seems clear that the changes in the way we receive and distribute information will affect our perception of ourselves as audiences, adjust our relations with institutions and organizations, and guide our approach as public-relations practitioners.

We begin with some general questions. As far as public relations is concerned, it may be a much less certain world. Access to once-private information, the ability to communicate, and to be communicated to, could be near-universal. Will we then have need of public-relations specialists? Large quantities of 'raw' data and news already falls instantly into our hands whenever we choose. What need shall we have of people to interpret it for us and to act as brokers responding with messages on our behalf? Might not communications between audiences and organizations become more open, honest and direct, freed from the expensive intervention of public relations?

This change in the way we deal with communications, sporadic as it may occasionally appear, belongs to an existing theme – a series of observable reforms stretching back to Swift and described earlier. We have explored some of the drastic changes humans have engineered to the speed of message delivery and the contradictory ways they have altered the expectations of their audiences. Tennyson, the poetic spirit of the Victorian age, wrote excitedly of this onward leap in *Locksley Hall*: 'Not in vain the distance beacons. Forward, forward let us range/Let the great world spin for ever down the ringing grooves of change.' Much of the forward movement has been determined by communications. We are experiencing 'the annihilation of distance'.[3] Peary's cable from the Arctic Circle to the banqueting journalists in Copenhagen, besides telling us something about hype, vindicates the respect that modern public-relations methods must pay to the authorities of time and space. From stage coaches to e-mail, the application of increased velocity to the transportation of physical or intellectual goods from A to B has forced us, the audience, to rethink the ways in which we communicate and respond to communications.

So what will the promised arrival of several hundred television channels, let alone the multiplication of radio stations and newspapers, do for our powers of concentration, a feeling of shared identity with others, a commitment to local communities? We will continue to encounter fellow humanity in the flesh in certain spaces: hospitals, sports stadia, shops, but in the main the frequency of those encounters will be reduced. Many more of us will work and communicate with the entire world from our homes, and as a result to retreat into them for longer periods. We may have more freedom about whom we choose to meet. Will that make us more or less tolerant? More or less open to alternative messages? 'Better fifty years of Europe than a cycle of Cathay', urged Tennyson. But the pace and the disorientation is having its effect on our minds and outlook as public relations audiences. Our outlook and expectations seem to shift and shift back again within the space of fifty hours, let alone fifty years – disconcerting enough to make a cycle of Cathay sound like the more comfortable option were it not for the fact that thanks to Hong Kong Cathay itself is now embarking on the same cycle as Europe.

Some people are worried about the implications of intensive communications. From the perspective of public relations, the two greatest fears are of coercion and subversion. Coercion from Big Brother, as foreseen by George Orwell in *1984*, through enhanced powers of observation and communication controlled by the State? Or subversion from the fringe? Does the use of electronic networks by extreme political groups or paedophiles across Europe imply anything about the future direction of the communications revolution? Elsewhere, corporations, governments and pressure groups incessantly monitor, research and chatter down the information highway: to us and to themselves.

What seems certain from all this is that the audience – us – is going to change, in a period as significant for humanity as the Reformation and the industrial revolution. We will not face 'at last' our 'relations with our kind' as Marx predicted, because an absolute end will not be reached. Communications will force us to adjust those relations again and again. It may radically complete the process launched through those two events, and fracture communities into temporary clusters of free-roaming, momentarily connecting, individuals. Or it may merely change our perception of audience: from largely geographic and historic – based on shared proximity; to electronic – based on shared, specialized, interests and networks. We will be a less certain and secure audience. We might not be able to look forward to the same degree of individual protection as seemed briefly possible for many in the post-war world. Old age pensions, even health protection will seem worryingly inadequate in relation to our expectations. Few of us will know the security of a single job for life, and some will blossom amid the choices. We will seize the chance to work more independently, but we will keenly feel the uncertainties of irregular employment. Perhaps we shall spend many hours alone, stewing in small pools of light behind our screens, in touch with the world but experiencing little physical, daily, contact with other people and the organizations that may occasionally employ us. Without an office at which to spend most of the day, the circle of our physical human contacts may be as limited as it was for our isolated rural ancestors. Many of us may take an interest in our immediate community; others, able to restrict their contacts to those with whom they feel a shared cultural, racial or sexual affinity, may grow more sensitive to outside intrusions and quicker to feel intolerance or offence; those who choose not to connect with others outside the family or immediate community may struggle with person-to-person contact. They may instead choose to communicate on their own terms, through the images created by artificial reality. It may be that these people will be less prepared for the quirks and surprises that characterize un-idealized, real humans. The organizations that serve them may seem somewhat imperfect. At the same time, the increased dialogue over the ether will bring distant people into contact with one another, and open up new areas for intellectual exploration. The results may be mixed. We will, though, be highly absorbed in the possibilities of human technical achievement and therefore technologically aware, partly in order to be attractive in the job market. Meanwhile, others will feel nervous, powerless or exposed, at the mercy of a mass of machines. We may, if we are sensible, enrich our minds and lives, using the new technology to take a deeper interest in the world about us, in spiritual exploration or the arts and sciences. Some will try opting out of the system and others may foolishly attempt to cope with its excitements and demands by using mood-altering drugs. We are likely to be more mobile, and less likely to take on homes of our own. We will have different perceptions of what it means to be both in work and out of work. Others among us feel hurt, cynical and determined: perhaps feeling the tension between the expectations of our parents and grandparents and the fact that the world they have created makes those expectations difficult for us to realize. These persons may feel they owe no-one a living but themselves. We are the first of this audience, children and young adults, some entering university or at the start of their working lives.

As we change, so too will our attitudes towards the institutions that for the present claim to guide or provide for us. In these circumstances, how can any single organization hope to live up to the highly specialized expectations of millions of people? It cannot, and we must learn not to expect it to. Institutions themselves must change their functions and communications. Some – possibly including stationery, books, newspapers and the post office stamp – may become much less necessary to some of us. We will treat the others in a different way. Who will need to communicate to us? What will we have to say to each other? There will always be banks, manufacturers of goods, and governments. How will they make themselves known to us? Will government function through a computer terminal? Will it take the opportunity to provide us with instant democracy – the capacity for any of us to enter any public debate we wish and at the end of it cast an instant vote by the press of a button? Perhaps many of the issues we now reserve for the politicians alone will be left to us to decide. It will be difficult for governments, dependent on the network, to restrict access to the information they store on it – someone will be bound to break in. The prospect arises of politicians basing their relationship to the people on interpreting raw information that we all share, rather than on what they choose to withhold and to distribute; and, hopefully, not on the image created for them by carefully staged public events (because there will be no 'public' to stage them for) or meaningless speeches hammered clumsily together by teams of consultants (because universal access to the relevant information makes such speeches redundant). Of course, human nature will ensure that some people are more committed to public affairs than others; the others may be uninterested in new possibilities for shared debate, and ready to place their vote at the service of someone whose opinion they trust. If the voter can instantly gratify his or her desire for knowledge, he or she may have less to ask about. It may be possible for governments and politicians to devise persuasive new means of making themselves attractive – through virtual reality or carefully written interactive packages – and maintaining their role as public leaders rather than public servants. The access we might have to Government may pale in comparison with the access that it could have to us, say, justified on grounds of security. We may become the most monitored society in history: every aspect of our private lives – spending habits, personal communications, movements – may be readily accessible to the bureaucracy. What will it do with such information? Will its use be restricted solely to the pursuit of criminals?

How will non-government organizations employ this technology to advertise, to persuade, to defend themselves? When 'public pressure' mounts up in the near future, what form will it take? Perhaps a refusal to buy a company's products, electronically pre-arranged between thousands of people, who jam a company's electronic communications with instantaneously released protest messages. When people are moving from one organization to another, and less likely to spend time in its physical environment, they will require a fast means of introduction to the new organization's culture, outlook and other personnel. Many non-manufacturing organizations or departments may not need a 'physical' environment, and will exist electronically, through a web of connected employees marketing, selling, accounting, conducting legal work, transferring funds, staging annual general meetings via terminals, and deciding strategy – what sorts of communications will they need to consider to create a shared identity for employees, subscribers or customers? For those who continue to gather at common work spaces, to manufacture or build, the issues may differ. They may, for the first time since the industrial revolution began, find themselves in the minority of the adult working population. Once, the stay-at-homes were mainly unemployed, disabled, retired or raising families. Now, quite possibly, the workplace minority will be regarded in a somewhat different light. The badges of achievement or social status may in the future be awarded to those managing to remain at home; and changes in perceptions of 'home' as opposed to 'workplace' employment may have an effect on the way those in work view themselves, or select the organizations they work for. This, in turn, would require the communication of new themes by the affected organizations. A great responsibility will be placed on the people responsible for the new communications.

What is the likely nature of that responsibility? We should glance at the parallels between e-mail, cyberspace and the first, pre-industrial printing presses. The first printing presses appeared in Europe in the fifteenth century. They churned out the pamphlets that persuaded millions to accept the Reformation. An astonishing revolution in thought and outlook occurred, accelerated by an improvement in communications technology. 'Recent research suggests that the outpouring of tracts and pamphlets reached a peak during these years that was never again equalled.'[4] The coming communications revolution will become as prolific, and as accessible to any person or organization. Through its total availability, it might effect an equally massive change, as business – as close to our lives now as was the Church at the Reformation – is forced to step further and further away from the rational, technical perspective that dominates its activities, even to the point of putting altruistic acts of corporate social responsibility before the requirements of production. New messages are required to arm and educate new generations for this emerging world, and we are already beginning to seek out their possible content. Some of them are wrapped up with our desire to join the communications highway itself, rather than to raise any particular question or seek out any particular answer once we arrive on it.

It could consequently become more difficult for organizations to communicate their points of view. This is because the networked world will adjust our ideas about consent, and about collective action by motivated people. Of what value is 'public opinion' in a society of individuals laced together by fibres and capable of transmitting their opinion swiftly, easily and inexpensively to the exact person who needs to know about it? An organization's carefully researched public message may struggle painfully through the network but emerge into an electronic space emptied of collective expression; unread grafitti on a wall, more lifeless than the decorated cavern at Trois Frères. The next 'key influencers', the people who lead debate on specific issues, may only be those whose views momentarily dominate a computerized dialogue. They will be more difficult to identify than today's key influencers – the people who lead pressure groups into noisy public debate, hold meetings, arrange demonstrations, reserve to themselves the ability to establish connections with politicians and the media. In the near future, many more of us will be able to participate in deciding the fate of an issue, by talking to whomsoever we choose. Physically 'branded' high-publicity pressure groups may simply dissolve into joint actions and decisions taken by highly motivated but independent people. What, in a community of wired-up individuals, will become of that generator of public opinion, the mass media? In the terminal age, paper newspapers and magazines could become more select, with a smaller number of highly informed readers. They may transmit their written content through fibre-optics, and incorporate the possibilities of viewer interaction and virtual reality. Newpapers might turn the written word into a blend of written, spoken, and moving images.

Perhaps then public relations will be forced to rebuild itself on a principle that it and we have almost forgotten – that there is a profound human urge to communicate that exists regardless of changes to our physical world. Beyond the ambiguous requirements of the powerful, the complex and insatiable desires of the consumer, and the real or imagined grievances presented by a mass of opposing pressure groups, the information highway may in time cause us to retrace our steps in the search for fundamental contact with others, somewhere 'out there'. This is likely because the changes ahead will create a good deal of alienation and dislocation. Audiences and organizations uprooted from more-or-less familiar ways of doing things always seek to reinvent their needs and roles. Much communications work will be undertaken by organizations to reinvent their relationship with employees and key influencers. Messages about an organization's point of view on a problem, or a new service, must be aligned to each individual and, by ethical access to information about their preferences, to the virtually real, electronically connected or geographically traditional communities to which they choose to affiliate. Images and phrases will be customized to a currently unrealizable degree of detail. A prime theme in the uncertain society will be the communication of trust: trust us with this invasive technology; with the sensitivity to accommodate your idealistic beliefs to our operations; to take the decisions that will improve the quality of your lives. The power of communications will be available to all: public-relations practitioners may have the capacity to enter into a complex dialogue with their audiences. They may have no choice, because the power to decide the right moment for a message to reach its audience is even less likely to be under their control than it is now. The moment a message or a communications strategy leaves the practitioner's brain and enters the computer terminal it runs the risk of being found, and becoming instant public property. A crusading or inquisitive person will have the capacity to present the intended audience with an issue or a carefully thought-out programme before the communicators have finished planning it. At such moments, the careful construction of trust will be more important than ever.

What activities will occupy full-time communicators? They are certainly less likely to be writing and faxing mountains of press releases, making videos, creating brochures and pamphlets, staging events and branding physical merchandise. Nevertheless, the problems that such activities try to tackle will not all change. Companies will still need to find ways of communicating the superiority of their product and their good reputation, even though many customers may purchase their goods and services through a terminal. Charities and voluntary groups will still have to lobby, but in different ways. Institutions will still need to talk with audiences about the social impact of their activities, legislation or general elections. They will still try to cultivate contacts with key influencers and secure their endorsement, perhaps over the network. But the means and tools for communicating to much larger groups of people are going to change. A paperboard packaging company concerned about forthcoming recycling laws might advertise and lead a discussion over the computer network, inviting selected commentators, or anyone with a point of view, to question an expert 'panel', each sitting behind their own screens in different countries. The audience may be a group of executive 'mercenaries' or consultants, hired for a short-term project by the company, and who must be introduced to the company in a memorable and speedy way. It may be a politician preparing an interactive speech, or a communications strategy that encourages people to e-mail a protest. The new public relations will hopefully concentrate on the creation of meaning at a highly individual level. If nothing else, the sheer volume of communications and massive accessibility to information will compel public relations to demonstrate its ability to listen, and to engage in substantial discussion; real communications in a world of virtual reality. The language of structured communications will change. It will grow more intimate, personal and open to responses. It will recognize that the common denominator among the audience of the future is the ancient human need for contact and for the strength to understand and cope with change. These are old needs, now drifting away from the physical and intellectual certainties to which they have been attached for less than two centuries, and in search of secure moorings. It will be the task of the communicators to help supply belief, and to show modern audiences how to quickly find their bearings and make sense of new surroundings, how to grasp things from new perspectives, how to be adaptable. This will involve new approaches by organizations. The communicators themselves may speed society away from its short reliance on the subtle, rich ambiguities of the written word in communications, and restore to us a pre-literate age, framed by the comparatively crude but magical projections of the visual image. Faced by such prospects, we must hope for the birth of an arranged interplay of words and images, unlocking new possibilities for expression in public relations.

In a society dominated by the machinery of total communications, there will be a need for skilled communicators. From them we will learn a new sort of public relations, a new way of sending messages via new media. We will demand new relationships between audiences and organizations. So be it. The information revolution is succeeding the industrial revolution: do not communications specialists have a duty to partake of that revolution and to help shape and explain it? The act of public relations, which is the structuring of communications to others, could soon be the one collective act we all have in common. People need public relations to facilitate their progress, to enable the networked society to connect with itself, and above all else to produce the same informed, expressive spark that we have glimpsed producing successful moments of public relations, great and small, trivial or important, from the distant past to the changing present.

We should not nail ourselves so strongly to our humours and complexions. Our main talent lies in knowing how to adapt ourselves to a variety of customs. To keep ourselves bound by necessity to one single way of life is to be, but not to live. Souls are most beautiful when they show most variety and flexibility.

Michel de Montaigne[5]

NOTES

1   *Newsweek*, 11 April 1994. p 85.
2   Marx, Karl. *The Communist Manifesto* (1848) Paragraph 24, lines 6–14.
3   The phrase is Paul Johnson's.
4   Pettegree, Andrew (ed.) *The Early Reformation in Europe* (Cambridge, UK: Cambridge University Press, 1992) p 6.
5   de Montaigne, Michel. 'On three kinds of social intercourse'. *The Complete Essays*. (London: Penguin, 1991) p 922, trans. M. A. Screech.

Bibliography

The following selection embraces helpful English language publications on public relations, together with additional works that would repay close scrutiny.

Bernays, Edward L., *Crystallizing Public Opinion*, New York: Boni and Liveright, 1923.

Bernays, Edward L., *Engineering of Consent*, Philadelphia: 1947.

Black, Sam, *The Practice of Public Relations*, 4th ed., Oxford: Butterworth Heinemann, 1995.

Bruce, Brendan, *Images of Power: How The Image Makers Shape Our Leaders*, London: Kogan Page, 1992.

Carty, Francis Xavier, *Farewell to Hype: The Emergence of Real Public Relations*, Dublin: Able, 1992.

Cooke, Robert Allen, 'Danger signs of unethical behaviour: how to determine if your firm is at ethical risk', *Journal of Business Ethics*, **10**, 1991, pp 249–53.

Dougherty, Devon, *Crisis Communications: What Every Executive Needs to Know*, New York: Walker, 1992.

Dowling, Grahame R., *Corporate Reputations: Strategies for Developing the Corporate Brand*, London: Kogan Page, 1994.

Dozier, David M., 'Planning and evaluation in PR practice', *Public Relations Review*, **2**, Summer 1985, pp 17–25.

Foucault, Michel, *Politics, Philosophy, Culture: Interviews and Other Writings*, New York: Routledge, 1988.

Foucault, Michel, *Power/Knowledge: Selected Interviews and Other Writings, 1972.* Translated and edited by Colin Grant, New York: Pantheon Books, 1980.

Fuhrman, Candice Jacobson, *Publicity Stunt!: Great Staged Events That Made the News*, San Francisco: Chronicle Books, 1989.

Grant, M.L., 'Perceptions of propaganda in inter-war Britain: The development of government publicity in the domestic sphere', Oxford University, unpublished doctoral thesis, 1988.

Grunig, James E. & Hunt, Todd, *Managing Public Relations*, New York: Holt, 1984.

Grunig, James E. & Dozier, David M. (eds), *Excellence in Public Relations and Communication Management*, Hillsdale, NJ: Erlbaum Associates, 1992.

Hainsworth, Brad E., 'Ivy Lee and the German Dye Trust', *Public Relations Review*, **1**, Spring 1987.

Hart, Norman A. (ed.), *Strategic Public Relations*, Basingstoke: Macmillan Business, 1995.

Holtman, Robert B., *Napoleonic Propaganda*, Baton Rouge, USA: Louisiana State University Press, 1950.

Innis, Harold A., *Empire and Communications*, Toronto: University of Toronto Press, 1972. First published by Oxford University Press, 1950.

Jefkins, Frank, *Public Relations for Marketing Management*, London: Macmillan, 1978.

Jordan, Myron K., 'FDR's condemnation of electric utility public relations', *Public Relations Review*, **2**, Summer 1989, p 41.

Kahneman, David, Slovic, Paul, and Tversky, Amos (eds), *Judgement Under Uncertainty: Heuristics and Biases*, New York: Cambridge, 1982.

Lee, Ivy L., *Publicity: Some Of The Things It Is And Is Not,* New York: Industries Publishing, 1925.

Lee, Ivy L., 'The problem of international propaganda. A new technique necessary in developing understanding between nations', London: Occasional Papers, **3**, 3 July 1934.

Lesley, Philip, *How We Discommunicate,* New York: AMACOM, 1979.

McIntosh, Malcolm *et al.*, *Good Business? Case Studies in Corporate Social Responsibility*, Bristol: SAUS, 1993.

Phillips, David, *Evaluating Press Coverage: A Practical Press Coverage to Measurement and Cost Effectiveness*, London: Kogan Page, 1992.

Philo, Greg and the Glasgow University Media Group, *Politics, Media and Public Belief*, Glasgow: Glasgow University Media Group, 1993.

Sapolsky, Robert M. 'Measures of life', *The Sciences*, March–April 1994, pp 10–13.

Sells, Bill, 'What asbestos taught me about managing risk', *Harvard Business Review*, March–April 1994, pp 76–90.

Stone, Norman, *How to Manage Public Relations: Practical Guidelines for Effective PR Management*, London: McGraw-Hill, 1991.

Stout, Sunny, *PR for Results: What It Is and How to Use It*, Knebworth, UK: Spearhead Direct, 1994.

Theobald, Robin, *Business & The "Community": Some Observations on the Development of Corporate Sponsored Volunteering in Britain*, London: University of Westminster Press, 1993.

Travers-Healy, Tim, 'Public relations and propaganda – values compared', *IPRA Gold Paper,* **6**, April 1988.

Tversky, Amos, 'Rational choice and the framing of decisions', *Journal of Business*, **4**, 1986, pp 251–78.

Webber, Alan M., 'The Statesman as CEO: an interview with Helmut Schmidt', *Harvard Business Review*, July–August 1986.

White, Jon, *How to Understand and Manage Public Relations*, London: Business Books, 1991.

White, Jon & Mazur, Laura, *Strategic Ccommunications Management: Making Public Relations Work*, London: Economist Intelligence Unit, 1995.

Wragg, David W., *The Public Relations Handbook*, Oxford: Blackwell Business, 1992.

Index